The Cancer Code

The Cancer Code

How a journey through leukemia
led to software that changed
the way people work.

Mike and Bettina Jetter
with Hobart Swan

Design: Kate Thompson, DillonThompson

Editor: Constance Hale

Copy Editor: Mandy Erickson

Library of Congress Control Number: 2003097196

ISBN: 0-9745598-0-6

Your purchase of *The Cancer Code* supports patients, families, medical teams and researchers in the fight against leukemia. A portion of the proceeds from this book will be donated to non-profit organizations in the United States and Germany that fund and support leukemia research.

What lies behind us and what lies before us are small matters compared to what lies within us.

—Emerson

Contents

The Triathlon

The New Beginning

"This is a success story both from a medical and from a business point of view. Mike is struck at a very young age by chronic myeloid leukemia, a disease which, until not too long ago, was uniformly fatal. He and his wife Bettina relate to us their story from Mike's diagnosis, to his transplant, to ... the development of a successful software company, and to the 'transplantation' of both of them from Bavaria to San Francisco to be part of the action in cyberage. They pay tribute to Mike's physicians, Dr. Kolb and Dr. Ledderose in Munich, who carried out the transplant, and in this context tell a bit of transplantation history.

The Cancer Code is told with great immediacy and, despite all setbacks and frustrations along the road, with contagious enthusiasm."

Dr. Joachim Deeg

Fred Hutchinson Cancer Research Center
Seattle, Washington

Physicians are obliged to strive for objectivity. In the struggle for the survival of our leukemia patients, we need a kind of emotional distance. We learn this professional attitude during our medical education, and this is often a long and painful process. But emotional distance provides a necessary wall of protection.

Reading Michael and Bettina Jetter's story tears this wall down. Irresistibly, we are drawn into this tale of suffering, struggle and final recovery from a deadly disease. In every passage of the text, and in between the lines, we feel deeply touched by the intensity of a wide range of human emotions: fear, sadness, anger, persistence, hope, trust, bravery, and patience. Michael and Bettina's family and friends are equally moving and impressive in their support, courage, and love. What more can a brother do to show his affection than by donating his own life-saving bone marrow?

Michael Jetter's story fills us with gratitude for our scientific predecessors and co-workers. To have bone marrow transplantation as an effective tool against leukemia is a great achievement. Every effort in improving this treatment is justified and rewarding. We are proud and grateful that we here in Munich are able to show that immune cells of the donor can cure a dangerous recurrence of deadly leukemia following bone marrow transplantation. This seemingly simple but fascinatingly effective treatment was wonderfully successful with Michael Jetter.

While *The Cancer Code* reads like a novel, it is anything but. Michael and Bettina Jetter's story is true in a deep sense. Only those who have personally endured a struggle for survival could write a book like this. We thank the Jetters on behalf of our patients. This book will give them hope and strength.

Prof. H. J. Kolb   Dr. G. Ledderose

José-Carreras Transplantationseinheit
Klinikum Grosshadern
Munich

The Cancer Code

the challenge

The Heist

ULI WASN'T USED TO DRIVING A STATION WAGON and crunched the front of the Passat into a pile of snow at the end of the parking space. February's first cold front had dropped more than ten inches over Munich the night before. The hospital's maintenance crew had worked all morning like barbers, deftly shaving the snow off the asphalt to the edges of the parking lot. Then an unseasonably warm day sent rivulets draining back into the lot. By now, eight o'clock on Friday night, strands of ice stretched across the blacktop like a spider web.

Finally parked, Uli emerged from the driver's side of the car while Bettina, clutching a parcel, opened the passenger door. Together, Uli and Bettina, my sister and my wife, stepped gingerly to the main entrance, commandeered an elevator to the third floor, and marched to my room to liberate me.

I had shared a corner room with an elderly patient since I had been admitted five days earlier, on January 28, 1990. I had seen his puffy, pale-bluish face only in the rare moments when the curtains surrounding our beds were parted at the same time, but we had never spoken. I had gathered from conversations that he was suffering from a heart condition and was now in the midst of a bout of pneumonia.

Over his bed hung an assortment of beeping, whirring, and clicking devices brought in to monitor his fragile health. The night before, I slept fitfully as he hacked and coughed, weakly trying to expel the fluid collecting in his lungs.

Our large metal beds stood against the wall, between them an old double-hung window covered with beige venetian blinds, the slats of which were closed now to block out the lights from the surrounding office buildings. By each bed stood a single stainless steel nightstand. My roommate's was empty. Mine held a clock, a glass of water, my Walkman, and two computer magazines.

I had awoken that morning to an orderly telling me to get out of bed so that he could change my sheets. I had already complained to the doctors about this—about being treated as if I were perfectly healthy. Since the moment I was admitted, my only respite from the sharp, clawing pains that racked my leg had been one shot of morphine. But after a half-dozen neurological tests, blood screens, and X-rays, the doctors were unable to pinpoint the location of the pain. Word seemed to have gotten out to the hospital staff that the guy up in room 305 was faking it.

So I was not in a good mood when my attending physician burst into the room on morning rounds. With a patronizing tone, he announced that they would not be conducting any more tests and, frankly, didn't really know what to do with me. Unlike my roommate's suffering, which clearly emanated from a bad heart, my leg pain, he declared, was all in my mind.

That did it. When Bettina visited me at lunch, I told her in no uncertain terms that if I had to spend twenty-four hours a day in unremitting agony only to hear some either incompetent or uncaring physician dismiss my pain, I was going to jump out the third-story window.

Six hours later, there she was, at the side of my bed, with a getaway car and a driver.

Quietly, so as not to disturb my roommate, Bettina and Uli slipped through the curtain around my bed, gave me little pecks on the cheek, and whispered to get up and get dressed. Bettina opened the parcel she had brought, pulled out a box of chocolate, and passed it among the three of us.

As I leaned unsteadily against the bed in my T-shirt and boxer shorts eating chocolate, Bettina and Uli crouched down to slip sweat pants onto my bad leg. It was at this moment that we heard the night nurse padding into the room.

After a perfunctory pause to ask if she could come in and take my temperature, the nurse drew back the curtain, took in the scene before her, and asked us what we thought we were doing.

"What we should have done days ago," Uli calmly replied.

"We're getting my brother out of here." Uli was an acupuncturist and physical therapist who had spent much of her professional life at odds with Western medicine. As such, she was not easily intimidated by medical professionals. "We need to find someone who actually knows how to care for him," she told the nurse.

"You've got a lot of nerve saying something like that," the nurse said, then turned and bolted out the door.

Uli, older than me by two years, has a face that reflects the contradictions she embodies. She has our mother's prominent cheekbones and laugh lines—not to mention her love of people, warmth, and spirituality. The jutting chin, straight, strong nose, and planar eyebrows come from our father and manifest her capacity for intense focus, her persistence, and her stubbornness. She had used a combination of all these traits to help many patients extricate themselves from a German national health care system that she considered overly regimented, invasive, and insensitive. Now it was her time to help me.

Bettina and I were still novices at dealing with the medical profession. With the occasional bruise from skiing or sprained ankle from hiking, we had had only passing contact with doctors and hospitals. Bettina wanted to get me out as quickly as possible, but was unsure exactly what that entailed and had turned to my sister for help.

Bettina and Uli had just helped me into my parka when a doctor I'd never seen rushed into the room, the nurse at his heels. He was a florid man with a full head of wavy gray hair and an unkempt black beard. Annoyed at this interruption of the smooth functioning of his ward, his frown pushed his small wire-rimmed glasses halfway down his nose.

"You can't just walk into a hospital in the middle of the night and sneak patients out the back door," he said sternly. "If the patient wants to leave, there are certain steps to be followed."

Uli slowly wrapped a plaid scarf around my neck, then turned to face her accuser. Patients, she explained, are free to do what they think is in their own best interest. In fact, she said, they are obligated to do so.

Exactly how, the doctor asked, could patients be expected to know what was in their best interest?

Uli said something in reply, and as the argument grew more heated, the nurse ushered the two of them into the hall and away from my frail roommate.

Unnerved by the confrontation, Bettina occupied herself by gathering my belongings. She pulled my toothbrush, toothpaste, and comb from the nightstand drawer, swept up the computer magazines and my Walkman, stuffed everything into her purse, and tossed the bag onto her shoulder. All business, she put her right shoulder under my left arm, put her arm around my back, lifted me up, and said "OK. Let's go."

Ten minutes later, after negotiating the treacherous parking lot, we made it to the car. The two of them stretched me out in back— with pillows under my head and a blanket to keep me warm.

For the next three weeks, that station wagon became my personal ambulance. Bettina and Uli drove me from physician to physician, from CAT scan to electrified hot bath. Hobbling on my crutches, I sojourned from alternative medicine clinics to acupuncture specialists—even to one mysterious "wonder doctor"—looking for someone or something to stop the pain. It didn't occur to me then that the pain in my leg was a superficial manifestation of my real affliction. ▪

Silent Night

SIX WEEKS BEFORE THE GETAWAY, pain was the furthest thing from my mind. At that point I was in England on a business trip that would become a milestone in my professional life. I had traveled to Basingstoke with two colleagues from a company called Softlab to fix a software installation for the English Tax Revenue Agency. This was my first trip to England, and I had heard from friends that the city of ninety thousand an hour south of London was a great place to start. The Basingstoke Canal, dug in 1778 to ferry grains and produce into London, was considered one of the most beautiful waterways in England. The town itself offered trendy restaurants and a lively nightlife.

We saw very little of either canals or clubs. First there was the fog from the canal, which obliterated all local landmarks and transported us to the dank, eerie setting of a Sherlock Holmes murder. Then there was the endless work—ten to twelve hours a day in a windowless room that held the agency's mainframe computers. In spite of all this, I felt that the trip somehow marked a shift in my life.

After my supervisor was called back to Munich, I managed to stumble through detailed technical descriptions in my burgeoning English. I began to sense the possibilities of a career as a highly skilled software consultant willing to travel. I would tour the world solving the most baffling software problems and righting programming wrongs. I would wearily return to my wife and our home overlooking the wooded shores of Lake Starnberg and, farther off, the jutting peaks of the Alps.

On December 24, the day after returning from Basingstoke, I was flush with such plans as Bettina and I picked up my parents and drove under a gray sky past empty forests of black, leafless trees for a special Christmas service at our church in downtown Munich.

A twenty-foot Christmas tree, draped with construction-paper

chains made by the Sunday school students, stood adjacent to the pul-
pit. Garlands of fresh evergreen boughs and holly leaves festooned
the pews. Three or four dozen children, all dressed in their Christmas
best, crowded into the choir loft. With faltering voices and approxi-
mate harmonies, they sang carols that drifted up into the hidden
recesses of the church, barely visible in the roseate glow of the
stained-glass windows.

As much as we looked forward to hearing these angelic voices
once a year, our family was always anxious to return home to begin
our own Christmas Eve rituals. Barely an hour after we had arrived at
church, we were in our car and headed back south to Icking, a rural
town of about four thousand.

Built for my parents in 1969, our one-story white stucco house
in Icking had a large living room that faced a backyard, a dining area
set back into the foyer, and a small kitchen. Two of the four bedrooms,
the ones my brother and I had once occupied, were in the basement.

Only my twenty-nine-year-old brother Andi (for Andreas) wasn't
with us that night; Uli (Ulrike), twenty-eight, was, as were Bettina,
twenty-four, and me, almost twenty-six. We joined my mother in the
dining room while my father disappeared behind the carved double
doors to the living room.

As my father put the final touches on the tree, we nibbled on
pickled herring and beets in sour cream and swapped "Andi" stories—my brother's penalty for staying home in Switzerland that year
with his wife. We laughed about Christmas Eves past, when Andi
would be thrown into a dither because he still hadn't finished making
our gifts. One year, he made stars from sheets of colored paper, each
intricately folded then glued together around a central hub that contained a battery-powered light. It would have been hard enough to do
just one, but Andi decided to make five—one for each of us in the
family, including himself. After my father would call to tell Andi to
hurry up, my brother would stomp up the stairs and lecture us about
how handmade gifts took time.

Finally, Dad pushed open the double doors and invited us in.
Chains of shiny construction paper draped the walls from picture to
picture. My mother's collections of seasonal dishes were placed
strategically around the room, filled with sugar cookies frosted red

and green, or sprinkled with chocolate. The tree was in the center of the room—illuminated by candles that Dad had wired onto the branches. The light reflected in the plate-glass windows that looked out onto the snowy yard.

A fire blazed in the hearth, on which hung a dozen etchings of ancient bridges, a collection my mother had started thirty years ago in Rome. The seminal piece was of a young man in tunic and leggings reposing against a river stone and sketching the Pons Fabricus, a pre-Christian bridge that to this day crosses the Tiber River.

Glasses of wine in hand, we all settled back into the burgundy sofa and chairs and began opening gifts.

As we sat there chatting, I started to feel pain on my left side and my back. No matter how I shifted and squirmed, I couldn't find any position that lessened the dull ache. Bettina kept looking my way quizzically, finally asking if I was all right. I told her that I must have pulled a muscle exercising that morning. But it didn't feel like that kind of pain. It felt deeper.

After an hour or so, I told Bettina sotto voce that I wanted to leave. We bid hasty good-byes and drove back to the apartment we rented above her parents' house. By the time I climbed slowly into bed, my skin felt clammy and I was wincing with every breath.

I managed to fall asleep around midnight. But about four in the morning Christmas Day, I awoke in intense pain. I frantically told Bettina that I needed to see a doctor right away. We got dressed and sped to the nearest hospital. In the emergency examination room, the doctor gave me a quick once-over, took some blood samples, ordered a few labs tests, gave me an ultrasound, and disappeared down a hallway.

About an hour later, a different physician approached and told me that the test results were inconclusive: my white cell count was abnormally elevated, but it was not clear why. I would need to go to another Munich facility.

It was about 7:00 a.m. when we entered the second hospital. Once again I was shuffled off to a treatment room, where a new set of doctors and nurses began another series of tests. I must have been alone in the room an hour when one of the physicians walked in, closed the door, and studied me.

"How old are you?" he said.

"I'll be twenty-six in March," I replied.

"You look like you're in pretty good shape. What do you do for a living?"

"I'm a computer engineer."

"I have a nephew who does that too," he said, pausing again.

"I'm afraid that you have cancer," he said, "I want you to know that it is treatable—but serious. It's called chronic myeloid leukemia."

Hearing this, I lay back and stared at the ceiling. I actually felt calmer than I had since the pain first began twelve hours earlier. There was an explanation, if unclear, for this unbelievable pain. If there was a cause, I reasoned, there was a cure—so I would be fine.

The doctor finished telling me a few basic facts about the disease, and the nurse went to get Bettina. I carefully watched for her reaction, fearing that if she broke down in tears I would, too. She came into the room and stood next to the bed as the doctor repeated the diagnosis. She turned to me in confusion, then looked back at the doctor and said, "But how did he get it? He was perfectly healthy twenty-four hours ago."

― # Up from the Basement

I HAD BEEN PERFECTLY HEALTHY not just yesterday, but my entire life. As had my mother, father, sister, and brother. As had three of my grandparents. My grandmothers had lived into their nineties and my paternal grandfather, a minister, into his eighties. Only my mother's father had died in his seventies.

Everyone in my family had always been energetic and athletic. As a young girl, my mother, Lydia, played field hockey and dreamed of touring Europe in a Mercedes convertible. My father, Roland Jetter, was a skier and rower and lusted after world travel. They had met in the 1960s when my father had taken his first job as a construction engineer in Rome, where Lydia was working as a librarian. They fell in love and, before long, had their first child, Andi. Sharing a love of adventure, they jumped when Roland was offered a job managing a bridge-building project in Venezuela. Uli was born in Maracaibo. By the time I was born, we had moved back to Germany, to a small town outside of Düsseldorf.

My earliest memories are of the admittedly idyllic vacations we would spend in little farmhouses down south in Bavaria. As part of the vacation package, guests would help their farmer hosts with the chores. City-bound children like us were usually thrilled to herd cows and collect fresh eggs. But I never was much of a farmhand. While my brother and sister were running after the cows and cradling warm eggs, I would be inside disassembling old clocks my parents had packed for me. I rarely managed to put these things back together again. I just enjoyed methodically spreading the little parts all over the floor and pondering all the different ways they might fit together.

When I was six years old, my father accepted a transfer to Munich and moved us into our newly built house in Icking. I soon became involved in organized sports—soccer, basketball, volleyball—and did a fair amount of skiing. But I spent most of my free time in my basement bedroom studying mathematics, physics, and music. My family tells me that I was basically a recluse, wrapped up in my studies and my electronics experiments.

When I reached my teens, I came out of my shell and graduated from dismantling appliances to building speakers and amplifiers. In fact, I gained some local fame when I transformed an old electric piano into the first music synthesizer anyone in the area had ever seen.

My brief career as a musician began in 1981, when I was seventeen and a senior at Icking's high school. One day I saw an ad for a guitarist posted on a school bulletin board by someone from the nearby town of Percha. Although I was a pianist, I answered the ad and was soon playing lead guitar.

The band chose me for two main reasons: I had, first of all, a valid driver's license and access to a car. For a band of sixteen-year-olds who otherwise had to depend on their parents for transportation, my availability as a driver covered a multitude of guitar-playing sins. I also had the distinction of being the only person to respond to the ad.

Once I joined the band, I soon got all the electronics practice I could ask for: repairing our speakers as fast as we could blow them out. I soon became the leader of the band, due, I suppose, to my seniority as well as to my obsessive personality. I pushed everyone to practice more and secured better-paid engagements. Before long, I was convinced we had a chance to make it big. But first, I had to fulfill my duty to my country. Before setting off on a fifteen-month tour of duty in the army, I decided to throw myself a big going-away party. That party changed my life. ▪

4 ─ A Boatman's Daughter

IN MY FAVORITE PHOTOGRAPH of my mother and father, they are standing in their backyard in Percha, dressed in traditional finery and about to attend the seven hundred fiftieth birthday of the church whose steeple loomed above their home.

My father, Josef, wears his fancy embroidered lederhosen, the dress-up version of the leather pants that used to be worn every day by local farmers. (Tourists often mistake lederhosen for costumes, not realizing that they are warm, durable, and, like blue jeans, apt to become more comfortable with age.) My mother, Theresa, is wearing a hand-embroidered dirndl.

Mike's family moved around, but my family had stood very still. For the past five generations, my father's family, the Paulis, has lived in Percha, a village of about two thousand residents on the shores of Lake Starnberg. When I was growing up, my parents were active in the local shooting club, a very traditional Bavarian form of social life. They also organized the village's cart races and belonged to the ski club.

My father was also a member of the city "council" (though it was not as formal as its American counterpart) and of the team that each year reenacts the centuries-old Bavarian tradition of the maypole (*Maibaum*). Every four or five years, a group of townsmen go off into the woods in search of a tall, straight tree to represent the community. Once they find the perfect specimen, they cut it down, strip off its bark, paint it in the traditional Bavarian blue-and-white stripes, attach wood or metal images symbolizing the life of the village—then plunk it down in the middle of the town square. If, at any point, men from the nearest town are able to sneak in and steal the pole, the town must pay to get it back—and host a big party for the thieves and their village. This ancient ritual is followed by towns as small as five or ten farmhouses and as large as Munich, whose maypole towers more than a hundred and fifty feet over the city's ancient *Viktualienmarkt*.

Like his father before him, my father had spent his entire adult life working on the ferries that carry tourists across Lake Starnberg. In the summer, he was a ferry captain. In the winter when the boats were still, he changed hats and became a carpenter, responsible for maintaining all of the woodwork aboard the ferries.

While my father was off tending boats, my mother tended to the family. I am the eldest of three daughters, but once had a brother two years younger. Named after my father, Joséf was born with a heart abnormality, and when he was six, before he started his first full year of school, he underwent a risky heart surgery which he didn't survive.

Perhaps because of some unconscious desire to be the son my father lost, I have always been somewhat of a tomboy. While Mike was down in his basement tinkering, I was out doing what his father probably wished Mike was doing: hiking in the woods or the Alps, wind surfing and sailing on Lake Starnberg, taking long bike rides— doing anything to stay outside for as much of the day as possible.

Because the busy time of year for my father was in the summer when tourists descended on Lake Starnberg, we took most of our family vacations in the winter. This was fine with me: one thing my father and I shared was a love of skiing. We could never afford lavish vacations, but a little more than an hour away was some of the best skiing in the world.

In summers, while my father was ferrying tourists, my mother and I visited my grandparents' farm in rural Bavaria. I learned to drive trucks and tractors, feed the cows without getting my toes crushed by their hooves, and stand on a rickety ladder in the autumn wind while picking my weight in apples and piling them into a canvas bag strapped to my shoulders. ■

THE DOCTORS TOLD ME that chronic myeloid leukemia (CML) was a "mild" form of leukemia. I soon came to learn that that was not quite true. All the different kinds of leukemia break down into two main forms. The "acute" form targets children and older people, starts quickly, and must be treated aggressively—primarily with chemotherapy. Survival is usually less than one year. The "chronic" form tends to be more common among middle-aged people. But while chronic myeloid leukemia takes longer to develop, it is just as hard to treat—and just as deadly.

CML evolves from an abnormality in stem cells in the bone marrow. When strands of two different kinds of chromosomes inside stem cells break, the broken ends then attach to each other form a new, abnormal and relatively easy-to-detect chromosome called the Philadelphia (Ph) chromosome (after the city in which it was discovered). The chromosome derails the normal function of bone marrow and initiates an uncontrolled reproduction of all types of white blood cells and platelets (which help blood clot). At the same time, new stem cells are created that contain the same cancer gene—and the process accelerates until the bone marrow effectively shuts down. Once it does, the patient experiences severe internal bleeding, overwhelming infection, anemia, and, finally, heart failure.

As a first step in treating the leukemia, I was put on a drug called hydroxyurea that the doctors said would reduce the stabbing pain in my side. This pain, they said, was caused by an enlarged spleen, the half-pound, fist-shaped organ that is tucked away neatly on top of the diaphragm and under the left rib cage. In addition to producing and storing blood cells, the spleen is responsible for filtering blood before it flows to the liver, removing such things as bacteria and defective cells.

The Philadelphia chromosome was signaling to my marrow to produce white cells like a runaway assembly line, rocketing my blood count past the normal four to eight thousand cells per cubic microliter to more than two hundred thousand per microliter. With fifty times the normal number of white cells to remove, my spleen was swollen and tender. With no room to spare, each time I exhaled, my diaphragm rose up and mashed my spleen into my ribs. This was part of the pain that drove me to the hospital on Christmas Day 1989. I could breathe in. I just couldn't breathe out.

By interrupting the signal to my marrow, the hydroxyurea would slow the production of white blood cells, shrink my spleen, and relieve the pain. It was a good drug for relieving the symptoms, but wouldn't cure the disease.

By evening on December 25, already feeling the results of the hydroxyurea, I lay in my hospital bed and wondered how I could have suddenly become so ill. As the hours crept by, I realized that perhaps the onset of the disease wasn't as sudden as I wanted to admit. I had started to notice earlier in the fall that my overall health was declining. I was running out of breath more easily. I had lost most of my appetite and was losing weight. And I had had night sweats a couple of times. But I just ignored these signs. I told myself that I was working too hard and not paying enough attention to exercise—probably drinking too much coffee as well. Maybe I had known all along that there was something going on, but just couldn't face it. Until it became impossible to ignore.

On my second day in the hospital, the doctors told me that they wanted a clearer picture of how far the leukemia had progressed. They said they needed to do an immediate biopsy of my pelvic bone in order to measure the number of Ph chromosomes in the marrow.

The problem with these biopsies, they said, was that the pelvic bone couldn't be numbed. The doctors needed to go in and literally cut little cylinders out of bone, but wouldn't be able to give me anesthesia.

The procedure was incredibly painful. It required three doctors to complete the biopsy: one to hold my legs, one to hold my arms, and another to manipulate the tool that cut the cylinders. As I lay there trying to cope with the physical pain, a thought occurred to me for the first time: This disease might not simply cause me pain. It might kill me.

On the third day my doctors listed my options.

Because I had two siblings, the best treatment was to undergo what was known as allogeneic ("from another") bone marrow transplantation[1], in which physicians harvest healthy bone marrow from one person and infuse it into another. At the time, this was the only course of treatment that offered any significant hope of curing CML. It also had the lowest rate of survival of my three options. As with any procedure that involves the introduction of foreign tissue into a body, allogeneic transplant posed the great risk that my body might reject the marrow, even if it came from my brother or sister.

Hardly sanguine, my physicians warned that, despite fifty years of research elsewhere in the world, the use of bone marrow transplants in Germany to cure leukemia was still very new. German doctors had begun just five years earlier to become familiar with the bone marrow transplantation procedure and to determine which types of leukemia it was best used for.

Bettina and I considered traveling to Seattle to have the transplant done by the leading experts. But even back in the 1980s, it was an exorbitantly expensive procedure, costing in the neighborhood of

---

[1] In 1939, American physicians led by Dr. E. Donnell Thomas had attempted, unsuccessfully, to inject a few milliliters of foreign bone marrow into a patient. After World War II, research began again, funded by the American Atomic Energy Commission. The United States government, in attempting to prepare for a nuclear disaster, opened a new door in leukemia research. The canine subjects in the Atomic Energy studies had been given massive doses of radiation to see how much their bodies could withstand. Leukemia patients were irradiated in order to kill off malignant cells. The canine and human subjects died—not because the foreign marrow couldn't live in their bodies, but because the patients' immune systems attacked and destroyed the marrow.

Medical researchers were so discouraged by their failures that they abandoned the allogeneic bone marrow transplants among humans in the early 1960s.

Thanks to advances in kidney transplantation, however, scientists soon began to understand the mechanism that caused the recipient's body to reject allogeneic marrow. By 1967, leading bone marrow researchers determined that they had sufficient understanding of how to both perform the transplant and prevent rejection: it was time once again to try the procedure on humans.

In March 1969, Dr. Thomas and his team of physicians from the Fred Hutchinson Cancer Research Center and the University of Washington in Seattle performed the first successful bone marrow transplant using a matched sibling donor for a patient with advanced leukemia. Thomas went on to win a Nobel Prize in Medicine for his work in this field.

$400,000. As a German citizen, I could get the treatment in Munich for virtually nothing. Bettina and I tried to find data on bone marrow transplants done in Germany. What little we found was preliminary and vague. Only much later, long after I had had the procedure, did we learn that the survival rate one year after the procedure was between 5 and 50 percent.[2]

My second best choice was allopathic ("from the same") bone marrow transplant, usually performed when no matching donor could be found. In this scenario, the patient's own bone marrow is harvested, preserved by freezing, then reinjected after the patient's own diseased marrow has been destroyed by a combination of radiation treatment and chemotherapy. The main advantage to this course of treatment was that it precluded the rejection of foreign marrow by the patient's body. But it brought with it the risk of relapse. If Ph chromosomes in my blood survived and were reinjected into my bloodstream, I would be right back where I started.

The least dangerous and least hopeful path was to continue with the hydroxyurea. The drug would keep my white blood cells in check, but would not cure the disease. By taking hydroxyurea every day, I could probably enjoy three to eight more years of relatively normal life. But at some point the drug would become ineffective; my white blood cell count would climb out of control, destroying my bone marrow function, and I would die.

If I were to choose the allogeneic bone marrow transplant, the first thing I would need was a matching donor. At this time, there were no bone marrow databases in Europe. Then, as now, the best chance of finding a donor is to look among your siblings, with whom there is about a 25 percent chance of a match. Parents are also a possibility, but far less likely. Others outside the immediate family have only a one in twenty thousand chance of matching. Without a bone marrow database, leukemia patients circa 1990 who did not have matching siblings were basically looking for a needle in a haystack.

---

[2] There is still not a 100 percent cure rate for chronic myeloid leukemia. (The use of a drug called Gleevec does show promise of significantly improving cure rates.) But thanks to improvements in treatment, survival rates one year after CML bone marrow transplants have now risen to 80 percent.

There was a good chance that either Andi or Uli would be a match—but nothing was guaranteed. They were both tested, though, and I was greatly relieved to learn that Andi was a strong candidate for a match. More tests would be needed, but the odds looked good.

Ten days had now passed since I first reported to the Munich hospital and took my first dose of hydroxyurea. On January 3, my team of physicians decided to put me on a second drug called interferon alpha, considered an experimental treatment.

Interferon alpha is a protein normally produced by the body during viral infections such as flu. Interferon alpha, though new, was viewed as a kind of miracle drug, able to put the body into a state of high alert to fight sickness. Physicians had only recently begun using it for leukemia, yet there were early reports that some patients were going into full remission. CML researchers hoped that the drug might someday preclude transplants altogether.

But interferon has its down side. First, it is a natural substance that must be extracted from sheep using a very complex procedure. As a result, it is expensive. It also produces the same side effects as the flu, including chills, fever, muscle and joint pains, and fatigue. Some patients also experience hair loss, depression, and even disorientation or confusion following injections. Finally, unlike hydroxyurea, which is a pill patients can swallow, interferon has to be injected each day. Sure enough, during the night after the first interferon injection, I developed a fever and broke into a sweat. These symptoms subsided after an hour or so. Then I got the chills and shivered for hours more.

Fortunately, my system was able to adjust to interferon, and after three or four days these symptoms disappeared. This adaptability was good news in the short run. But it meant that in the long term I had to continually increase the dosage to get the same effect. Each time the dose was increased, the flu symptoms returned.

I ended up staying in the hospital for about four weeks. By the end of January 1990, my condition had stabilized and, with my hydroxyurea, my syringes, and a supply of interferon alpha in hand, I was discharged.

With a hospital staff no longer a buzzer away, Bettina was nominated to give me my interferon shots. A few days before my discharge a nurse had shown her how to do it, and had told her to practice with an orange. She did well with the fruit, but found it difficult to give me my first shot—which had to be administered directly into my abdomen.

Despite the shots, I felt confident about my chances. The hydroxyurea was relieving my pain, I had three decent treatment alternatives, and—who knew—maybe I would be one of those lucky people whose leukemia would melt away in the face of interferon alpha.

One week out of the hospital, severe pains in my leg sent me running—or rather, limping—back in to the hospital. That is, until Bettina and Uli got me out. ■

Club Atari

BETTINA AND I HAD BEEN MARRIED a year and a half by the time she and Uli rescued me from my hospital room. That experience can't have been what she envisioned the night eight years earlier at the going-away party I threw before my tour in the army, when she had beelined through the crowd for the kitchen, walked up to the woman she had already decided would be her future mother-in-law, and said, "Hi. I'm Bettina."

We met a few minutes later. As quickly as my father had years before, I fell in love. When my band mates shouted to me that it was time to perform, I pulled myself away from her and found my guitar. It occurred to me then that the last thing I wanted to do was stand around playing music with a bunch of guys—not to mention spending the next year or so in the army.

For the first three months of my military career, I was assigned to a base about a hundred miles away from Icking. Before long, though, I managed to get transferred to a post just a few miles from Percha. From this point on, every evening I would leave the base, hitchhike into town, and spend the evening with Bettina. Long after I'm sure he would have liked to have been sound asleep in bed, Bettina's dad would get up and drive me back to the base.

My duties as a soldier were light. Bettina had begun an internship at a local bank. She was seventeen. I was nineteen. It felt like we had all the time in the world to get to know each other.

In the fall of 1983, my military obligations fulfilled, I immediately began my next "tour of duty" at the technical university in Munich, where I enrolled as a student in the mathematics of electronics. It was a very demanding course of studies: of 725 original classmates, only 250 were left at graduation. I was relieved to be among them.

But as someone whose interest in electronics grew from taking apart clocks and building synthesizers, I soon found the coursework too theoretical. I was learning how to build things like radio transmission towers, which was interesting—but I was doing it all on paper. Using mathematical formulas, the class would compute the perfect height of the tower, the perfect diameter of the dish. As a fellow student put it: "You can design all you want, but once the thing gets built you always have to take out a hammer and give it a whack to get it to work right."

That kind of real-world problem solving interested me much more than sitting at a desk fiddling with a calculator. It's not that I didn't understand the value of theory. I understood that when you designed a new kind of airplane you couldn't just construct a few planes and see which ones fell out of the sky. I just realized I no longer wanted to be the one stuck in the room figuring everything out in advance.

And so in 1984, as I entered my sophomore year, I switched to the computer science program and began studying things like network diagramming and CPU architecture. Soon I was reading all the books and magazines I could find on the emerging world of personal computers.

It was around this time that Atari brought out its first series of personal computers (PCs) with graphical interfaces such as garbage cans and printer icons. I remember thinking that this was the greatest thing in the world. Macintosh was the only other computer with a graphic interface. Without a Mac or a PC, anyone who wanted to do something on a computer had to know how to program—how to use strings of characters and symbols to initiate action.

At this time, Microsoft was nine years old and Bill Gates and his friends were still developing MS DOS. Others were either programming in Basic, which was considered a lightweight language, or in FORTRAN, Pascal, or COBOL. The former was too simple to program complex instructions; the latter had to be used with expensive workstations.

The Atari system, on the other hand, was programmed in C, which filled the gap between the other languages. But it was new. To appeal to reluctant buyers, Atari sold its PCs at a very attractive price—an amount even we students could afford. My friends at the university and I were so thrilled at being able to buy our own PCs that we founded the first German Atari users' club three months before the computers were available on the market.

Because our group became involved with Atari so early in the product lifecycle, we were able to make direct connections to company programmers. This meant we could get our hands on software development kits—thick manuals that explained in detail how to write programs for the Atari. We traded manuals and spent endless late nights in smoke-filled Munich cafés and dormitory rooms poring over them and sharing our dreams about the fantastic applications we would someday design.

Similar to the Macs, Ataris presented users with a number of graphical symbols. By clicking on these icons, users could do things like open applications and check available memory—actions that otherwise had to be initiated by typing in strings of computer commands.

Neither Macs nor Ataris looked like anything that had ever been seen on a computer screen. They were easier for nontechnical users to understand, but were still very rough. We decided that it would be our mission in life to transform this nascent graphic interface into something powerful and elegant.

I immediately started developing applications for the Atari, working as a contractor for a software company. My very first application was an astronomy program for creating horoscopes. It contained my first animations: planets that spun around as they crossed the screen. At first, I was proud of the program and even made a bit of money. But I quickly grew bored and wanted to do more complex programming, which meant that I would have to go back to nongraphical programming.

When the astronomy company contacted me a year later and said it needed new add-ons to the horoscope tool, I had lost interest in spinning planets. To get them to stop bothering me with something so mundane, I quoted a price so high I figured they would hire someone else. Their response: "OK, when can you start?"

Switching from theoretical mathematics to programming looked like a good career move. ■

the marathon

The Golden Gate

WHEN THE TIME CAME for Mike to enter the army, it was time for me—or rather, my parents—to choose my educational future. The choices included a vocational track, which led to a job in the trades; apprenticeship training with a company followed by a short "university" education for those planning a career in commerce; or the full college track to prepare a student "for anything."

I didn't have a strong preference for any of the three. Given my family background, the idea of going to a full-fledged college was foreign. So my parents chose to put me on the second track, advising me to "Choose something where you can earn some money, something that is stable, where you think the company will be around for the next twenty years."

So in the fall of 1982, I started my career at the savings bank in Starnberg. For the first three years, I was moved around from department to department so that I could learn a bit about the different aspects of the banking business. After this training period, I was assigned to staff the bank's board of directors. Three years after that, I asked to be reassigned to the bank's marketing department, which seemed exciting and creative.

Over the next few years, I would work in the marketing departments of ever larger companies, finally ending my marketing career at the French fragrance corporation Clarins, where my responsibilities were developing strong management and leadership skills.

In the summer of 1988, after Mike had received his degree and started his job at Softlab, we were married at an old church on a hill overlooking Lake Starnberg.

The next morning, we embarked on a four-week honeymoon, a tour across the great American West in an RV. We logged thousands of miles, starting in New York and traveling to the Grand Tetons, the

Grand Canyon, the Sierra mountain range, and downtown Los Angeles before setting our sights for San Francisco.

Once we arrived, we squeezed our mobile home into our hotel's underground garage and spent the next few days seeing the city by foot, by cable car, by bus, and by the Bay Area's underground railway system.

I couldn't go back to Percha without being able to describe to my father the local ferry system. So one morning we took a cable car down to the wharf and jumped on a ferry headed north past the Golden Gate Bridge, past Alcatraz and Angel Island, and on to the Marin County town of Tiburon.

As we sat in a waterfront café sipping cappuccinos, we saw a man about our age, dressed in an Italian business suit, zoom up to the ferry terminal on a red Vespa. Slamming on the brakes, he jumped off the scooter, slung a plastic backpack over his shoulder, and ran down the dock to catch the ferry. Mike and I looked at each other. We didn't say a word. But we were both thinking the same thing: Wouldn't this be a cool place to live?

We had our family, friends, and careers waiting for us back home. But maybe some day we'd be back. Then came the diagnosis.

BY MARCH 1990, I had spent a month in the hospital and three weeks riding around in the back of my parent's station wagon as Bettina, Uli, and I fruitlessly searched for relief from the pain. As the scenery and the time rushed past, I began to think that maybe the doctors were right after all. Maybe the pain really was all in my head. So when one those same doctors I had run from recommended that I join a group therapy session to investigate the psychological side of disease, I figured I had nothing left to lose.

One overcast morning, Uli piled me into the back of the car and headed around Lake Starnberg for Bernried Castle, set in a secluded park against the lake. Bettina, not yet ready to accept that my pain might, indeed, be psychological, stayed behind. But here Uli was in her own element. She had been a great help since my leg pain began, first visiting me in the hospital, then confronting the doctors and getting me out, and finally locating alternative healers. Having studied alternative medicine, she had thought all along about the mind-body relationship and its role in my pain. Now that I was receptive to the idea, she was there for me again.

I had never been very close to Uli. Being older, she liked to boss me around. Then she had gone off on her own and challenged all the social conventions I had since embraced—not settling down, not seriously pursuing a career. She was a peace activist and a feminist, and always seemed to be at war with something—politicians, the legal system, the medical establishment. She was, it seemed to me most of the time, against everything.

But the more I hung around Uli, the more she helped me stand up to the medical establishment and find answers to my own questions, the more I felt like she really understood me—and the more I understood her. For the first time, I began to feel comfortable around her. With Bettina still skeptical about unconventional treatments, Uli was the only person to whom I could express hopes and fears about the therapeutic approach.

There were nine other people in the therapy group, which was led by a woman named Karin Fuersich. Three were cancer patients. One was an alcoholic. I couldn't figure out what, if anything, was wrong with the others.

Karin was of average height and stocky. Her mane of flaming red hair, her complete self-confidence, and her utter belief in the ability of individuals to re-create the world according to their needs (she had even reinvented her last name, which means "for me"), made her seem like a force of nature.

We spent the first two days talking as a group, creating some paintings, and trying to get to know each other. But on the third day, we took turns standing up before the whole group. This was when Karin showed her uncanny ability to penetrate to the core of our defenses—to challenge us to make the changes necessary to alter our lives. One by one we would stand there in the center. One by one, she would reduce us to tears, of either anger or sadness. Before long, each of us had grasped our reasons for being there.

When I stood again in the center, I felt able to talk more and more openly about my disease. But Karin said I was intellectualizing, not feeling. Yes, I could recount my story. Yes, I could cite leukemia survival rates and treatment options. But I was in complete denial, she said, that I had a mortal disease.

On the morning of the fourth day, Karin asked me to stand in front of the group. I was tired of the pain and feeling pressure from the others. Looking at me sagging between the crutches I had used since I left the hospital, Karin asked how long it would take for me to do something dramatic, to put aside my intellectualism and break through the mental logjam. I glared at her for a moment then, in defiance I suppose, threw my crutches down and started hobbling around in circles, swearing at the crutches the whole time.

After about two turns around the circle, I noticed that the pain had lessened, so I quieted down and returned to my seat. At the end of the session, Karin suggested that I leave the crutches where they lay in the center of the circle. I never used them again.

Subsequent conversations with Karin helped me understand that after taking the drugs that relieved the pain in my spleen, I had passed the first month feeling healthy enough to avoid the reality of my disease. This denial was made easier by the fact that, in some respects, chronic myeloid leukemia is a breed apart from other cancers. Unlike, for example, breast cancer and lung cancer, each of which has a "home" in the body, leukemia is everywhere and nowhere. There is nowhere you can point to and say "That's where it hurts, doc." Absent great pain, she said, it was easy for my conscious mind to forget that I was sick at all.

It was as if my subconscious mind had decided to locate my cancer in my leg in order to force my conscious mind to face my diagnosis—as if it were saying "Not sure if you are really ill? How about this pain? Does that make it feel real enough?" For an engineer with a belief in a rational world, the sudden appearance—and equally sudden disappearance—of such intense, real pain was a revelation. From this moment on, I understood very clearly that I would need to manage both the illness and how I felt about the illness. My illness.

Thanks to the German health insurance system, I had not had to work since I was first hospitalized at the end of December, 1989. In May 1990, Bettina and I decided to take a short vacation to Lago di Garda in northern Italy. We spent two days relaxing in a hotel high above the lake. We would wake late and drink our cappuccinos outside on the hotel terrace. Then we'd lean against the stone parapet, pumping lira into the stationary telescope and peering at the castles and villas jutting out of the thick forests below. During the day, we would wander along forest trails or go window shopping in the lakeside village of Limone. At night, we'd dine at the hotel or in town, read, and go to bed.

But on the morning of the third day, I awoke with new pains—this time in my chest. By the afternoon, the pain became so severe that we packed our things and headed back to Munich. I still remember the car ride home. Normally it seems like the trip home is faster. Not this time. No matter how fast Bettina drove, it seemed like time had come to a halt. For five hours, I squirmed and writhed inside our small car, trying desperately to find a position where the pain was less intense.

MIKE

As we drove north, I kept bouncing back and forth between two possible explanations. I had just learned that physical pain, however real, could be psychosomatic. On the other hand, I had heard a lot of horror stories. In the four months since I had been released from the hospital, I had had to return once a week for blood tests. Each time, there would be at least three or four other CML patients in the waiting room. Some were like me: on some kind of drug treatment. Others were preparing to have the bone marrow transplant. Still others had come out the other side and were in recovery. With time on our hands, we would all sit around and tell each other stories.

I couldn't stop thinking about the other patients—not the ones who had no hair or who had some horrible skin condition; not the ones who looked pale and gaunt from some unanticipated drug interaction; not the ones who had defeated the disease. I thought about the ones who never made it. What if we got back to Munich and the doctors told me, "Well, look, Mike. These new pains are very real. Your condition has deteriorated dramatically. There's not much else we can do for you."

Contributing to these fears was my lack of knowledge about the disease. Thus far in my interactions with physicians and patients alike, I really hadn't asked too many questions. At the same time, there simply was not a lot of information around about possible complications of CML and its treatment. What existed was in English and very difficult to understand. I also had a fundamentally fatalistic attitude: if a thousand complications were possible and each leukemia patient's situation was unique, if no one knew what really worked and why, then what good would it do for me to know anything at all? I was resigned to hear the worst.

Once we arrived in Munich, however, I was surprised—and relieved—to learn that my chest pains were nothing more than a side effect of too much interferon alpha. This turned out to be both good news and bad news.

The good news was that it would be easy to make the pain go away. The doctors simply needed to lower the amount Bettina injected each day. The bad news was that the chest pains weren't a promising response to a drug that had sent others into remission. Interferon alpha might cure me yet, but the chest pains were not a good sign.

Reducing the interferon dosage put my body in less of a state of high alert and caused my white cell count to rise once again. In response, the doctors increased my hydroxyurea dosage. But no matter how much the doctors reduced the interferon dosage, the chest pains continued. The doctors decided that it would be best for me to stop the interferon altogether and rely solely for a time on hydroxyurea. Once my system cleared out the interferon, they reasoned, I could slowly start taking it again.

Because both drugs lowered my white blood cell count, it didn't matter too much in that respect which drug I used. But the hydroxyurea didn't have the same beneficial effects on my immune system as the interferon. If I was to hold the leukemia at bay, I needed the interferon. My problem was that I was just one of those people whose systems, for whatever reason, couldn't take it in high doses for very long. Interferon might have been the perfect cure for me. But I would never be able to take enough of it to find out. It was time to consider my other choices. ■

9 — Choose Your Poison

ONE MORNING IN JUNE 1990, Mike and I pulled our car off the highway from Starnberg and headed for the looming white edifice of the Universitätsklinik Grosshadern. With fifteen stories of sheer concrete walls and an orderly façade of small, square unadorned windows, the hospital dominated the southern Munich skyline.

We parked on the west side of the building, entered, and descended two floors into a long, low-ceilinged hallway. Against one wall of the stark corridor, dozens of bicycles alternated with anonymous green metals doors. On the opposite side, rows of lockers led to a random stainless steel table on wheels, perhaps a portable medicine cabinet. A low but continuous rumbling sound came from somewhere on the floor—maybe a trash compactor or a furnace.

Our footsteps echoed above the distant clamor. When the hallway ended, we turned left, pushing through double doors to the brightly lit reception area of Station L21—the leukemia ward. I stuck my head into a small office and announced that we had come to see Professor Dr. Kolb.

In the six months since his initial diagnosis, Mike had been going to another Munich hospital that, while it treated leukemia patients, had neither the facilities nor the expertise to help us pursue either of the two remaining options. Mike would now need to have surgery. If Andi turned out to be a viable marrow donor, Mike would get an allogeneic transplant. If not, Mike would have to take his chances with his own marrow. After endless rounds of paperwork, Mike was accepted into the leukemia program at the Universitätsklinik Grosshadern, one of four hospitals in Germany that could perform either of these transplants.

We stood in the reception area until Dr. Kolb came out to meet us. In his late forties, with dark brown, thinning hair, he was dressed in a blue-striped shirt and teal necktie under a pressed lab coat. He shepherded us into his cramped, windowless office and gestured to two molded black plastic chairs. His desk was neatly covered with manila files and various documents, many of which were lying open and stacked on top of each other.

As a young physician, Dr. Kolb had been one of the first members of Germany's medical community to get excited about the bone marrow research going on in the United States. He had spent much of his early career creating the hospital's leukemia program. He started in 1979 with one bed for CML patients. By 1982 his center had two beds. In 1989 the new ward was completed, giving Kolb six, then eight, then ten beds. By that time, the idea of using bone marrow transplants to cure chronic myeloid leukemia was seen as a viable treatment in Germany, and L21 had a long line of CML patients hoping to be treated.

Despite having since become something of an éminence grise in the field of bone marrow transplants, and despite his program having gained international recognition for its clinical work, Dr. Kolb struck us as both down to earth and compassionate. But over the course of the next fifteen minutes, our meeting would devolve into one long series of interruptions. Doctors would pull him out into the hall for consultations. Staff would come in to remind him of upcoming meetings or request his signature. While we found it very hard to concentrate, Dr. Kolb seemed hardly to notice, immediately returning his attention to us the moment the interruption ended.

In his swivel chair, he seemed to come alive like a professor expounding on his pet theory as he delved into the details of Mike's case. His clear, blue eyes seemed to lose their fatigue as he told us that he had reviewed Mike's medical history and was concerned about the amount of time that had passed since the diagnosis. Surely, he said indignantly, the doctors at the other hospital understood that the success rate for bone marrow transplants improved the sooner the transplants were performed—preferably no more than six months from the original diagnosis. Knowing that Mike was past that point, Dr. Kolb wanted to begin treatment right away and had, in fact, already assembled a team of doctors and nurses.

He told us that there was room for Mike in his program right now—but that that could change at any minute: the leukemia ward was obligated to admit those who needed treatment the most. He said that Mike's best chance clearly was to get the transplant, but that there were no guarantees. If Mike stayed on hydroxyurea, Dr. Kolb reminded us, he could be reasonably sure he'd enjoy as many as eight or ten more years of relatively comfortable life. If we went ahead with the transplant, Mike might succumb to either the radiation therapy or the chemotherapy that would prepare him for the transplant. Or the transplant could fail. If we chose the transplant route, Mike could be dead in a matter of months.

Dr. Kolb paused to let that sink in then asked us quietly if we had any questions about the transplant. Was there any chance, I asked, that the radiation would make Mike sterile? He began slowly, carefully choosing his words. "We have had patients who have been able to have kids after five or ten years. But there isn't enough evidence yet to say for sure. Some of our patients have chosen to have their sperm frozen. But we still don't know if leukemia has a genetic component."

Dr. Kolb's office grew silent as Mike and I let those words sink in. We had always wanted a family. Were we willing to take the risk of never having children—or of giving birth to a child who might be born with some sort of disability?

Mike looked at me and I nodded. He turned to Dr. Kolb and said that we wanted to proceed with the transplant. In that case, Dr. Kolb said, we had better get ready. Mike would start the next day.

We left the hospital, drove home, and began calling our families and close friends, beginning the logistical and emotional preparations for the procedure. Everyone wanted to come over and comfort us, feed us, help us get ready to put Mike into the hospital. All we had the strength to do was to explain the situation to everyone and tell them we would contact them from the hospital when we knew more. Late that night, we finished packing a few things for Mike and tried to get some sleep.

But early the next morning, a nurse from Dr. Kolb's office called and told us that they were sorry to have gotten our hopes up, but we would have to wait. A much sicker patient had materialized the night before and needed the room.

Mike and I had no choice but to wait and see when the hospital would be able to fit him again. Following his hospital stay in January 1990, Mike hadn't gone back to work until May—and soon found the job too stressful. His supervisors at Softlab were very understanding and transferred him to a position where he didn't have as many responsibilities. But soon even that was too much. He quit Softlab in July and began working for another software development company, AKM.

We tried to focus on our jobs, but twice more that summer, the hospital called and told us that a room had opened up. Each time, we went through the parting ritual. Each time, we were told at the last minute that a more acute patient had appeared and would need the room.

By the end of August, we were at wit's end. We had spent the entire summer trying to control the nausea that welled up every time the phone rang: Was it the hospital calling to offer Mike a room? Or to take back one that had been offered? Was it a friend asking anxiously for news? Or a family member exhorting us to be more aggressive, to demand a room?

Each day that passed without any such calls seemed like a small miracle. But we also knew that that much more sand had passed through the hourglass—that Mike's chances of survival had slipped a few grains more.

All the while, Dr. Kolb urged us to remain flexible.

Then one day, Mike called him and dropped a bombshell: he was taking himself off the waiting list for three months.

This seemed utterly preposterous to Dr. Kolb. Every day counted at this stage of the disease. Yes, the waiting was hard. But to lose three months just because we were tired of the uncertainty would only further reduce Mike's already diminished chances of survival.

We were adamant. We felt like we had lost complete control over our lives. We had both become tired and morose, fearful of what each day would bring. Was this really the mental state Mike wanted to be in when and if he finally began this risky operation?

With a three-month hiatus from this uncertainty, we could focus on getting Mike into the kind of mental and physical shape that would give him the very best chance of surviving the cure.

Against his better judgment, Dr. Kolb accepted our decision. But he told us that even if we voluntarily made room for others on the list, the hospital couldn't give us any kind of preferential treatment once we wanted to get back in. Three months from now, we would have to wait our turn just as we had thus far.

Before Mike put himself out of reach of the program, Dr. Kolb had decided that it would be prudent to harvest some of Mike's own marrow in case an allopathic transplant was required.

Even though we knew from preliminary tests that Andi's bone marrow was a potential match, Dr. Kolb reminded us that more precise tests were still ahead. Even if the tests went well, he said, there was no guarantee that, once injected into Mike's body, the foreign marrow would be accepted. By that time, the doctors would already have destroyed all of the Mike's own marrow. If Andi's marrow was rejected, the only way the doctors could save Mike's life would be by reinfusing the marrow he set aside now.

When Mike and I first learned that the most promising cure was something called a bone marrow transplant, we both conjured up images of some gruesome procedure in which surgeons would have to saw open Mike's bones to access the marrow.

But the harvesting of bone marrow was a relatively simple procedure that took about two hours. To harvest the requisite liter and a half of marrow, the physicians inserted a small syringe hundreds of times into Mike's pelvic bone, each time withdrawing a small amount of the thick, stem cell–rich blood.

Once the anesthesia wore off, the most painful side effect was that for the next week or so Mike didn't want to sit down. He was also tired from the blood loss. But his speedy recovery indicated that he was still quite healthy despite the cancer. The doctors assured us that the holes in his pelvic bone would soon be healed, his marrow regenerated, and his blood supply replenished. ■

The Bone Marrow Olympics

FROM THAT FIRST CHRISTMAS NIGHT when Bettina had rushed me to the hospital to getting my bone marrow harvested, nine months had elapsed. I had no more illusions about the seriousness of the challenge ahead.

Beginning in September, 1990, Bettina and I began developing a training program for what we jokingly called the Bone Marrow Olympics. We enlisted the help of Karin Fuersich, the same therapist who had helped me understand my leg pain.

One thing we had learned from talking with former patients was that the better physical shape patients were in prior to the transplant, the longer their bodies could endure the aggressive, damaging treatment.

First, I began following a vegetarian diet, as did Bettina. We put aside our native diet and its emphasis on *Wiener Schnitzel* and *Schweinebraten* and switched to more fresh fruits and vegetables and grains such as whole wheat pasta. I even enrolled in a Chinese cooking class to learn now to stir-fry vegetables and tofu.

Then l began a strict exercise regimen of Tai chi, squash, and aerobics. At Uli's suggestions, I also started getting Shiatsu to revitalize and relax my body. And I started getting Vitamin B injections and taking vitamins and minerals to fortify my blood.

Knowing only too well that I needed to pay attention to my mental and emotional health, I began practicing meditation and, with Karin's help, visualization exercises.

Professional athletes are among those sold on the value of visualization. Baseball pitchers will often sit quietly before a game and imagine every pitch they will throw to every batter. Olympic high jumpers visualize every step they will take in their approach to the bar, then imagine how they will twist and stretch to clear it. Similarly, I began learning how to visualize my body destroying the cancer.

One of the visualization exercises Karin taught me was to imagine something like a *Star Wars* episode in which the good guys, my good white blood cells, were flying around in little spaceships shooting down the bad guys, the Ph chromosomes. Before I went to sleep at night and again when I awoke in the morning, I would lie in bed for ten minutes and imagine this war of the worlds raging inside of me. It seemed silly at first, but was surprisingly effective at teaching me how to first sense and then strengthen the connection between my mind and my body.

Because Bettina and I liked to play squash, I also did visualization exercise on the courts after work. Bettina would shout at me to hit the ball like it was one of those cancer cells. This was great. Not only was I able to visualize beating this disease, but I could also release a lot of the frustration I was feeling. This was great therapy for me, and it had the added benefit of giving Bettina a good workout—probably much more than she bargained for. I was a pretty strong guy back then and would hit the balls so hard that Bettina had to move quickly or risk large round welts on her arms and legs.

When we first decided that I would do the transplant, Bettina and I imagined that our family and friends, of course, would be there to support us, dropping in to say hello, bringing me bouquets of flowers, and regaling me with news from the outside world. We were wrong.

Because I would soon have no immune system to speak of, I would be sequestered inside a tightly controlled, germ-free isolation room. Family and friends would pose serious, potentially life-threatening threats to my health. The runny noses, sore throats, and winter coughs; the chocolates, flowers, and chicken soup—even the clothes on their backs—would become as deadly a threat to me as a burning stick of dynamite.

Very few people would be allowed to visit me, and they would not come bearing gifts. I could not, for example, "waste my energy" by entertaining well-meaning guests who started off wishing me well and ended up moaning over faltering marriages, car accidents, or pink slips. We would need to be absolutely certain that all those who entered my little world understood very clearly that they were there to give, not take.

The need for this kind of certainty led to the creation of my Bone Marrow Olympics "training" team, a carefully chosen group of individuals whom we'd allow to visit while I was undergoing the treatment. Bettina would, of course, be the team "captain" and Karin would be the spiritual coach. But after that, choosing team members became more complicated.

Before my diagnosis, Uli and I were almost completely out of touch. The only times I saw her were on those rare occasions when she would drop by for a family gathering and invariably figure out a way to put everyone on edge by deriding some recent political decision or assigning blame for the latest environmental catastrophe. Now I wanted her right her at the center of my life.

She told me that she, too, was thankful that the leukemia had helped her connect with me. In her eyes, I had always been the distant one, the third child who had never been able to really connect with his older siblings—the one who perennially hid out in the basement laboratory.

Uli would be on the training team, as would Andi—assuming he passed the final bone marrow compatibility tests. But what about my parents? What role could they play? As it turned out, none at all—not at this stage.

We decided that I needed to exclude them simply because we knew that Roland and Lydia would be sick with worry over me. They would naturally want to know each day how I was feeling, if I was in pain. And we knew that I would not be able to be brutally frank and say "I feel awful today and am in a lot of pain and I am afraid I am going to die." I wouldn't want to worry them. So I would have to put on a brave face and tell them that I was fine, feeling great, brimming with confidence. Maintaining this charade would be too big a drain on my emotional resources. It could not be allowed.

My parents accepted this decision without protest. We learned later that they had constantly called anyone in contact with Bettina or me to find out anything they could. We also learned that Roland had religiously kept a diary of the events surrounding my transplant: everything he and Lydia thought and did, everyone they spoke to about me, everything these people said. When it was all over, in an action befitting a left-brained, dyed-in-the-wool engineer, my father gave everyone in the family a handsomely bound, type-set copy of the diary.

Bettina's parents, on the other hand, had never gotten nearly as involved in our lives. Had Bettina and I not lived for years in an apartment above them, I might never have had a chance to get to know them at all. (We had moved in two years earlier after our wedding.) Her parents had always counted on the rental income from the apartment, but they had let us stay there nearly rent free so we could save up enough money for a home of our own.

Their house occupied half of what was once a larger piece of property owned by Bettina's grandmother. On the other half lived her aunt. Set in the middle of Percha, the entire lot comprised about a half an acre, as did most of the lots in town. Her parent's half of the property was filled with fruit trees, flower and vegetable gardens, and a large patio.

The home had been designed to be rented, with the second floor completely separate from the first. We shared an entrance, which suited Bettina's parents, who were very private people. In the years we had lived above them, we did not socialize with them very much. Now that I had been diagnosed with cancer, we saw them even less.

It wasn't that her parents didn't care about us. I think it was just too emotionally draining for them to be around someone with cancer. But they showed their affection in other ways. We would often return from our days at work or at the hospital to find platters of food waiting for us at the bottom of the stairs—everything from freshly picked produce to fully prepared dinners.

In the end, Karin, Uli, and Bettina formed the core of the Bone Marrow Olympics training team. Then we signed up Reinhard (Reini) Klein, the best man at our wedding and one of my oldest friends. He was one of the few men in whom I felt safe confiding, to whom I could express my fears, and who always seemed to know the latest joke. A co-worker of mine at AKM, Christine Schramm, with her twinkling blue eyes and wry smile, would serve as a bridge to my colleagues.

The final member of the team, Dr. George Ledderose, was also the leader of another team, the one that Dr. Kolb had assembled back in June. Drs. Ledderose and Kolb, while they clearly shared a pro-

MIKE

found love of their work with leukemia patients, were otherwise a study in contrasts. Where Kolb was on the short side and built like a wrestler, Ledderose was tall, thin, and gangly. Kolb had a receding hairline, while Ledderose had a thick gray mane that he constantly pushed back off his forehead. While Kolb's office was cramped but neat, Ledderose's was cramped and chaotic. And if Kolb tended to be more obscure and professorial, Ledderose was straightforward and avuncular. We took an immediate liking to him.

It was Dr. Ledderose who asked Andi to come down from Zurich and complete the final round of testing to make sure his marrow was compatible. Two days later, we had the results: Andi was a match.

Besides the team of doctors and nurses assembled by Dr. Kolb and Dr. Ledderose—and the hospital orderlies who twice a day scrubbed down my room and changed my sheets and clothes—Andi and the members of the Bone Marrow Olympic Training Team would be the only other people allowed anywhere near me for eleven weeks.

Mind Mapping

PERHAPS BECAUSE WE FACED such an uncertain future, Mike and I will always remember the fall and winter of 1990—when we were ensconced in our snug apartment and focused on preparing Mike for his treatment by eating well and getting lots of rest and exercise—as one of the most fulfilling times in our lives. As we drew the support team together, we had neither the time nor the energy to maintain superficial relationships. Outside work, we saw only the people we really wanted to see, and found this kind of "controlled socializing" very refreshing. For the first time in our lives, it seemed, we were getting a sense of how we really wanted to live, of what was really important to us.

Something else had started to click for us. It was called "mind mapping." In the fall of 1990, we had been introduced to this new theory on learning and memory. In retrospect, the timing of the introduction seems almost pre-ordained—as if we were meant to learn about it at a time in our lives when we felt terribly fragile yet eager to learn about new ways of looking at the world.

Mike and I learned about mind mapping separately, through our respective jobs. German companies in the late 1980s had become very interested in teaching their employees how to think more creatively about business challenges. Mapping was one of the techniques often taught.

In the early 1970s, British memory expert Tony Buzan had started searching for a method to capture ideas in a way that would both stimulate creativity and improve a person's ability to remember. His solution was the technique of mind mapping, in which people would draw a kind of "information picture"—a combination of words or images that represented or referred somehow to the subject at hand. First, you drew a shape in the center of a sheet of paper and inside it wrote a title for your map. Then you would draw branches radiating from the center. On each branch you would add a word or an image that related to the subject at hand. To each branch, you would add more sub-branches and more images. When your mind map was complete, you would have a document that, according to Buzan's research, would appeal to the "whole brain."

Mind mapping, which was really a very benign, light-hearted, life-affirming approach to thinking, drew on brain research that had a fairly gruesome history. During the 1950s and 60s, physicians had landed upon a surgery known as commissurotomy to cure patients who suffered from severe, intractable epilepsy. In this procedure, the surgeon would open the patient's skull, lay back the brain's coverings, and expose the corpus callosum, a ganglion of nerve fibers that connects the two hemispheres of the brain. The surgeon would then snip through the front three-fourths of the corpus callosum, severing a pipe-cleaner-sized cross connection known as the anterior commissure but leaving intact the back of the corpus callosum, the splenium. By separating the two sides, the physicians reasoned, they could prevent the seizure from spreading to additional brain areas. Amazingly, this horrendous procedure not only lessened the seizures, but did so usually—but not always—without significant side effects.

In follow-up research for which he later was awarded a Nobel Prize, psychobiologist Roger Sperry discovered that commissurotomy created in a few "split brain" patients not just separate brains—but separate minds that often acted independent of each other in almost bizarre ways.

When one split-brain patient, for example, had an argument with his wife, he attacked her with his left hand and tried to protect her with his right. Another patient would try to pull up his pants with his right hand while his left hand tried to take them off. A third patient, "Paul S.," was an anomaly among patients in that his right brain, normally unable to construct many verbal responses, was able to articulate. Sperry and his colleagues "interviewed" each side of Paul's brain separately. When the researchers directed to his right brain the question of what he wanted to be, he replied that he wanted to be a race car driver. When they asked his "left" brain, he said he wanted to be a draftsman.

These patients were instrumental in helping Sperry and his team understand just how different the two sides of our brains were. With our corpus callosum intact, the two sides of the brain are able to send information back and forth, integrating these two diverse worlds and enabling us to "act normally."

Subsequent brain research has clearly identified the characteristics of each of our cerebral hemispheres. The left brain is now known to be the residence of logic, reason, mathematics, and language; it is where we learn to speak languages and read and write sentences. This is the side that people like my husband use to do very analytic, linear work like software programming, accounting, and architecture. I could almost hear his left brain grinding away some nights as he tried continuously and fruitlessly to fit the sudden appearance of his illness into the logical pattern of his life.

The right brain is now recognized as the hemisphere that synthesizes individual features into faces, that understands the rhythm of music and sees patterns in nature. It our creative side that "thinks" in terms of the whole that gathers in the gestalt. Standing in front of a Picasso, it is our right hemisphere that revels in the shapes and hues on the canvas, that integrates the shards of Duchamp's "Nude Descending a Staircase" into one elegant, fluid movement.

Buzan surmised that by creating documents that contained all of these elements—written language, spatial relationships, color, hierarchy, rhythm, and imagery—both sides of the brain would be stimulated. Once stimulated, our minds would naturally be more creative, more engaged.

For some reason, maybe simply because it provided an interesting diversion from the impending transplant, Mike and I both gravitated to mind mapping and began using it in our daily work.

In 1988 I had moved from the board of directors to the marketing department at the Starnberg bank—the same place I had worked in since my high school apprenticeship. Relieved of the drudgery of planning meeting agendas and taking board notes, I felt exhilarated by the change of pace. With marketing, I was able to release the creativity that I felt had been pent up my whole life—as if I had finally found my calling. Two years later I was introduced to mind mapping and became enthralled with this new technique that enabled me to,

BETTINA

as I told my co-workers at every opportunity, "work in a new, whole-brained way."

I drew mind maps of marketing campaigns to help me keep track of endless details. In one campaign, the bank invited one of the country's leading TV anchors to come and talk about Russia with the employees of one of our larger clients. To prepare for the event, I drew a map with branches to words: for "speaker" I used my box of colored pencils to draw a little TV and anchor next to it; for "location" I drew a sketch of the building where we would hold the event; for "To-Do list" I had more branches connecting words that reminded me to design the invitations, compare mailing prices, create guest lists, and so on.

I was also in charge of developing the teenage market. So I created maps to stimulate my thinking about ways the bank could reach out to young people.

Mike initially used the mapping technique for his software development work at Softlab, then further refined it at AKM. Mike found that the mapping structure was a great way for him to break down large software projects into smaller components. He would first map out the main features, break the features down into components, and the components into subsystems. Rather than ending up with a linear list of tasks, he would have a map that showed not just the tasks but how they related to each other and to the larger feature set. Gaining this overhead view proved to be a key advantage for him.

Mike had taken a risk when he took himself off the Universitätsklinik Grosshadern hospital waiting list because he felt he needed to prepare for the transplant. But as the fall of 1990 passed into winter, the procedure drifted further and further from our minds. Life seemed good—better, in fact, than it had seemed for some time. We soon found ourselves being tempted by an option we had rejected. Would it be so bad, we wondered, if Mike chose the pharmacological route? Mike's life might be shorter, but now that we could see a better way to live, maybe it would be enough. Weren't a few years of guaranteed happiness better than the slim hope of a full recovery?

Lulled by our newfound peace of mind, we hardly noticed the time slip by. Before we knew it, three months had passed, and Mike was back on the list. Barely a week later, the hospital called: Mike could enter the leukemia ward in six days—if we were still committed to the transplant procedure. We had to choose quickly before the space was given to someone else. We decided to go for it. ●

BETTINA

Blood Brothers

NOT SURPRISINGLY FOR TWO PEOPLE who shared something as intimate as the very marrow of their bones, Andi and I resembled each other physically as well. We were both lean and slightly muscular. We were both competent at sports. Of average height and weight, we both had straight brown hair, lots of freckles, and plenty of nervous energy.

But where I had chosen to lead a very interior life, both literally and figuratively, Andi was an extrovert in every sense of the word. While I preferred the lab, Andi loved the outdoors. He had become a landscape architect in Switzerland who counted Tina Turner among his clients. Where my world was small, filled with my wife, a small but close circle of friends and, increasingly, my family, Andi's world knew no bounds. With their newborn daughter, Viola, in tow, he and his wife were familiar faces in their church, constantly taking part in food campaigns and marches and other community events.

The Jetters of Zurich had even gained some local recognition. Their house in Zurich had a spare room in the basement that, through their connection with the church, was forever occupied by someone or other, drifting through town or through life, who needed shelter. Andi and his wife would never tell these people that it was time to move on: their guests were welcome to stay as long as they needed.

Everything Andi did spoke to his generosity of spirit. When I called him in January 1991 to tell him that I was about to enter the hospital to begin the transplant treatment, he quickly made arrangements to come to Munich.

As the donor, Andi would have to stay in the hospital from the moment my preconditioning started until about ten days later, when they would extract a portion of his marrow. It was absolutely critical to my survival that Andi remain in good health. Once preconditioning started and the radiation either destroyed or severely damaged my marrow, there was no going back. If Andi had an accident or became ill during this time and couldn't go into surgery, I would have to use my own diseased marrow instead. For the time being, his health was mine.

It was also time to mobilize the Bone Marrow Olympics Training Team. Uli, Reinhard, Christine, Karin, and Bettina made their own last-minute arrangements to take on their new responsibility of serving as my lifelines and liaisons to the outside world.

Never before had I packed so little to prepare for being away so long. On the other hand, I wouldn't be doing any sight-seeing or hiking. No fancy dinners or theater shows. No swimming or squash playing. My activities for the next three months would consist of lying in the middle of, and regularly pacing around, a very small, hermetically sealed room. My wardrobe would consist of sanitized blue hospital pants and shirt. I packed a toothbrush and hairbrush, but wouldn't need those for long. Almost immediately after starting the preconditioning phase of the treatment, my body would become too sensitive for toothpaste, toothbrushes, deodorant, shaving lotion, or soap—and I would soon lose all my hair.

Because I was not much of a reader, I packed my Walkman, some music CDs, and a handful of episodes of my favorite TV comedy show, *Alf*. If laughter really was the best medicine, I would need a major dose of it now.

Finally, late in the afternoon on Thursday, January 25th, 1991, more than a year after my initial diagnosis, I arrived at the hospital and checked in to Station L21.

When we got to the reception area, we were stunned to learn that Dr. Kolb had decided to delay my entrance into the ward. Because the doctors wouldn't be able to start preconditioning the next day as planned, Dr. Kolb told me that I could have a few more days of freedom outside. Come back on Sunday, he said, trying to sound cheerful.

This was good news in theory, but really very nerve-racking. I had just said good-bye to everyone and had mentally prepared myself to do the most difficult thing in my life. Now I had to do it all over again. To minimize the second round of farewells, we told only my family and a few friends that I was back. If there was one good thing about this delay, it was that I was able to spend some time with my brother—my donor.

Seventy-two hours later, back we drove to the hospital. This time I checked in to L21 to stay. The clock was ticking now. Bright and early the next morning, I was helped onto a gurney and rolled down a maze of hallways and elevators to the radiation clinic in the hospital basement to begin my preconditioning.

On the first official day of bone marrow therapy, Dr. Ledderose installed what is known as a Hickman catheter in my chest. During the course of my stay in the hospital, the medical team would inject a constant supply of medications and nutrients into my bloodstream. If they had to inject each drug with a needle, they would soon run out of injection points, making my arm look like a junkie's.

The Hickman is a small flexible tube that is stuck right into the chest and goes directly into the large vein that empties into the heart. This minor surgery takes about three hours and is normally done with local anesthesia. But Dr. Ledderose had a difficult time installing it in me. As he worked he gave me a hard time about being such a jock and having a big beefy chest "like Arnold." Normally, I wasn't quite so muscular. But I had spent so much time exercising to prepare for the transplant that Ledderose had a hard time getting the Hickman tube through my chest muscles. After much sweat and many jokes at my expense, he got the Hickman perfectly positioned, and there it stayed for the next three months.

On day two, the preconditioning began. Most people have had, at one time or another, the experience of being exposed to radiation— whether for the annual X-ray at the dentist's office or after breaking a bone. In these cases, the technicians drape you with a heavy lead apron to protect the rest of your body. Then they leave the room to protect themselves, and press a button that exposes you to a fraction of a second of radiation.

To start the process of killing all of my diseased bone marrow, however, my entire body would soon be exposed to radiation so strong it would feel like a breeze blowing across my skin. And not for just a second. Like some kind of giant microwave dinner, I would lie on my back in this basement room and be bombarded with intense radiation for thirty minutes, then turned over and baked for thirty minutes more. Before each turn, the technicians would spend fifteen to twenty minutes painstakingly placing my body at the perfect angle and distance from the radiation machine.

Each day for the next four days, I would lie in this room as still as possible, listening to my favorite CDs and feeling this toxic breeze blow across my flesh. The goal, each day, was to get through the treatment without "interruptions"—a polite way of saying "without the patient throwing up all over the place."

Happily, I made it through the first full session, two hours in total, without vomiting. I lay there as quiet as I could, feeling this deathly wind on my body and morbidly wondering what it was doing to me. The radiation wasn't painful—its destructive power wasn't that obvious. But when they brought me back to my room after this first treatment, I began to shiver uncontrollably. Later in the evening, the nausea and vomiting began.

At first, I tried to keep myself from throwing up. But I quickly figured out that the sooner I expelled whatever it was that had just invaded my body, the better I'd feel. Until the next treatment, that is.

I was physically ill and vomiting nearly all day long for the first two weeks. After that, it got somewhat better, but the nausea would linger throughout my three-month stay.

The treatments on the second, third, and fourth days of the preconditioning were basically the same as the first, and my condition worsened with each passing day. To prevent my vomiting during the treatment, the doctors gave me the latest anti-nausea drug, which they said worked far better than the previous one. And were they right. I took the new medicine before my next radiation treatment and although I became nauseated, I didn't need to vomit immediately.

After the second day, I began to suspect that this new drug was too good. I still became nauseous, but was not able to vomit no matter how hard I tried. This was good news in terms of keeping down the drugs I had taken orally. But it felt awful. I soon asked them to switch me back to the other medicine.

The nausea problem was somewhat mitigated when, after the second day, I stopped eating. That is to say, I no longer ate in the conventional sense of the word. It was now time in the process for me to begin receiving my nutritional needs via my Hickman catheter. With little except the medications to expel now, the first medicine worked well enough to get me through the rest of the radiation.

My teeth, throat, and stomach became vestigial parts of my digestive system as days, then weeks went by without my ever chewing or swallowing a thing. This was a true blessing. The bitter, burning taste that accompanies nausea is mainly due to stomach acids. But if you don't eat, you don't develop the acids. The nausea persists, but it becomes less traumatic with only medicines to purge.

And there were incredible amounts of medicines in there, especially for someone who normally thought twice about taking an aspirin. In order to combat infection, fungus, and a host of other potentially deadly eventualities, my medical team had me ingesting a dozen different pills each day.

I had acquired some practice taking lots of pills—vitamins and minerals—during the Bone Marrow Olympics' blood-fortification event. But one side effect of the radiation treatment is to dry up all the fluids that normally assist in the complex process of swallowing. Now deprived of those fluids, my throat had become sore and tender. The otherwise mundane task of taking oral medications had transfigured into some kind of horrifying circus trick like swallowing swords or driving nails up your nose. And then I had to keep the pills from coming back up again.

This goal of the preconditioning phase, which takes place during the first ten days in the hospital, is to apply enough lethal doses of radiation and chemotherapy to kill off the patient's bone marrow. By destroying the marrow, the doctors destroy the patient's immune system as well. This is all part of the plan: a successful transplant depends on the patient's immune system being sufficiently weak to not reject the donor's bone marrow.

But destroying the patient's marrow presents a problem. The marrow is where all the blood cells in our body are created—the white cells that fight infection, the red cells that carry oxygen in and carbon dioxide out, the plasma that carries proteins and sugars, the platelets that control clotting, and all the various other cells that keep us functioning. The life spans of these various blood parts vary, but none last longer than a few days—and many last no more than an hour. To meet its immediate needs, my body needed the marrow to be up and running. But for my long-term survival, I needed the marrow dead.

I received transfusions to replace lost red blood cells and platelets. The most worrisome aspect of this conundrum had to do with white-blood-cell production. Normally, the white-blood-cell count ranges from between four thousand and eight thousand cells per microliter of blood. After the pre-conditioning, however, the typical count is about a hundred cells per microliter. With virtually no white cells to fight infection, the immune system is almost totally disabled, and remains so until the donor's marrow begins to thrive in its new host sufficiently to re-create an immune system. But until this system is rebuilt, what would be the most minor infection for a healthy person can bring sudden death to the host. ▪

——(**Miracle Elixir**)

LEUKEMIA WARDS are designed to ward off infection, but this is not an easy task.

In the first place, while there are many ways to remove germs from the surrounding environment, even the healthiest body contains within it a frightening number of germs normally held in check by various blood cells. The staff of the hospital's Station L21 had to protect patients on two fronts: infection from within and from without.

To reduce the risk of environmental infection, the patient rooms in L21 were arranged down the short hallway of a structure that protruded from the main body of the hospital and into the surrounding woods. To get into the hall, staff and visitors alike first entered a small changing room that looked like a very small high school locker room. People would enter either individually or in a same-sex group, strip down to their underwear, change into sanitized blue hospital scrubs, and disinfect their hands. Then, in their stocking feet, they would pad out into the hall and choose from a free-standing rack a pair of disinfected white rubber clogs.

Before a physical object—whether eyeglasses, CDs, pens or a computer, keyboard, or mouse—could be brought into the wing, it had to be thoroughly wiped down with strong disinfectant.

A second layer of protection surrounded individual patients' rooms. Each room was equipped with an air lock, a system of double doors, and positive air pressure to ensure that each time the door opened, the air flowed out, not in.

My room was about twelve feet wide and fifteen feet long, with ten-foot ceilings and a small, tiled bathroom. Set into one wall was the airlock to the hall. The other held both a door and a large window to the outside through which I viewed the seasons, friends, and sometimes, it seemed, life passing by. Neither the outside door nor the window was, of course, ever opened during my stay.

The window faced south, bringing sunlight in on those occasions when a sunny day pierced the dreary German winter. But even then, since the growth of leukemic cells could be triggered by exposure to sunlight, the nurses were always quick to close the electric blinds lest the direct rays touch my fragile skin.

Compared with the ward where CML patients were treated just a couple of years earlier, my room was like a hotel suite. Previously, patients were housed in large plastic tents erected in the middle of a regular hospital room. The opera star José Carreras, for example, found himself in one such tent while being treated for acute myeloid leukemia in the same Seattle hospital that had pioneered bone marrow transplants two decades earlier. Between his fame and his fortune, Carreras had received the best care available on the planet—but even he got a tent. What had been state-of-the-art care just two years earlier already seemed by 1991 like an absurdly primitive contrivance. As much as it drove me insane to be trapped inside this little room for three months, I was thankful that I got the disease when I did. I've never cared much for camping.

Because the station was on the ground floor, I was able to see plants and flowers and the occasional bird. More times than not, I would simply lay in a stupor and watch endless phalanxes of steel gray clouds sweep by like the undersides of battleships.

Thankfully, the windows allowed me to engage in a modest amount of people watching. Not many pedestrians came this way. But I didn't need many. After seeing the same nurses and doctors over and over again, day after day, my heart would almost leap into my chest with excitement every time a "stranger" passed my window. I must have presented quite a sight to anyone who bothered to look inside. There I was, this bald, pasty skeleton with wild sunken eyes, cracked lips, and dull yellow teeth. I must have looked like a lunatic. No wonder people seemed to hurry past.

At the conclusion of the radiation treatments, I enjoyed one full day of rest before embarking on the next phase of preconditioning: three days of chemotherapy. Administering the chemotherapy drugs did not involve any complicated procedures. The drugs were simply added to the normal infusion of medicines, hydrating liquids, and nutritional compounds I was already receiving through my Hickman.

At first, I didn't feel any different with the addition to my ongoing drug cocktail. I remember foolishly thinking that this part of the treatment might be a breeze. Three hours later, the drugs kicked in. Three days of misery, filled with long bouts of nausea, now began.

After the chemotherapy, I was finished with preconditioning (or it was through with me). I had stopped eating. I was worn to a nubbin from all the vomiting and the drugs. But the good news was that my marrow had been destroyed. Oh, happy day.

The risk of infection peaks immediately following preconditioning, when the patient's immune system has been destroyed and a new one has yet to be created. For the next few weeks, everyone who entered my room had to add a heavy cloth surgery robe to their wardrobe. This final layer is added to try to shield the patient from germs the outer layer of hospital scrubs might have picked up outside the patient's room. Combined with the requisite latex gloves, the surgical face mask, and the hair cap, my visitors looked no more human than I did. For almost three months, the only noses, mouths, and cheeks I saw were those of the passersby outside. I never saw Bettina's face—and I made a habit of not looking in the mirror at mine.

While the staff of Station L21 was doing everything possible to minimize the risk of external infection, there remained the enemies within. The majority of the drugs I now took, antibiotic and antifungal medicines, were aimed at the life forms that live within all healthy individuals, the so-called commensals that normally do us no harm—held in check by our white blood cells. Most of these drugs were administered via Hickman. Others, such as the antibiotic Zovirex, were among the now twenty to thirty pills lined up on a tray on a small table next to my bed each morning. These I had to take orally.

Pill swallowing had long since passed beyond the merely impossible and into the realm of torture when something harder still came along—an astoundingly vile form of antifungal medicine.

For people with compromised immune systems, these internal fungi become public enemy number one. Unstopped, these normally nonlethal live forms can quickly lead to anything from toenail fungus to thrush to meningitis. As those with a crop of field mushrooms growing in their yards can attest, once fungi take hold, their spores are virtually impossible to contain. This is as true inside the body as on the front lawn.

My best defense was to deny the fungi a beachhead by taking a drug called Amphomoral. I will never forget that name as long as I live. Amphomoral is perhaps the most noxious, most repellant liquid ever created with human consumption in mind. Ingesting it was like trying to drink glue—extremely foul-tasting glue. But by gagging it down every morning I was applying to the inside of my mouth, the length of my esophagus, and the entirety of my stomach a physical barrier to the fungus, depriving it a toehold.

The normal dose for a healthy patient with a fungal infection was one pipette each day—about two or three milliliters. My dose was an entire bottle—equal to a couple of those miniature liquor bottles you get on airplanes. And for about the first two weeks of treatment, I managed to get this much orange gunk down my throat. But after that, I became like Marcel Proust, for whom the slightest scent of rusk bread would trigger memories from a distant past. For me, the memories were fresh and nauseating.

In the short time I had been at L21, I heard about other patients who had the same problem with the medicine. This made me feel slightly less guilty about not drinking every drop. Even so, I had to remind myself that Amphomoral wasn't some form of punishment concocted by depraved chemists. It was helping me stay alive. I couldn't bear to drink it, so I did the next best thing: I experimented with it, mixing in fluids such as juice, coke, and liquid chocolate. These made the drug more palatable, but only slightly so.

The doctors warned us about these soda fountain–like concoctions. In fact, this was the one point in my stay that I saw Dr. Kolb again with any frequency. It underscored the importance of preventing fungal infection to have Kolb himself put on all his gear and come into my room to admonish me to finish the bottle—and to drink it straight, no chaser. Adding ingredients, he was quick to point out, diminished the drug's adhesive strength and therefore its efficacy. But I think he was too much of a realist to protest too loudly: diluted medicine was better than no medicine at all.

It was a grand and beautiful day when, after about four weeks of experimentation, I found the miracle elixir. A splash or two of Schweppes Bitter Lemon made a Dixie cup of Amphomoral taste pretty good. The mixer's fizzy citric taste masked the monstrous stench enough for me to get down a good dose every day from then on.

Having survived both the radiation and the chemotherapy, I was now ready for the transplant. First, the doctors fed an enormous amount of liquids into the Hickman to wash the chemotherapy drugs out of my system.

On the next morning, February 14, 1991—Valentine's Day—Andi dropped by on his way to have his marrow harvested. What a way to show someone you care!

It was an odd sensation, lying there in bed, looking up at my brother, and musing how the tables could easily have been turned. I knew intellectually that what he was about to do amounted to little more than donating blood at the local Red Cross—and he would be anesthetized at that. But I just kept imagining all those people hidden behind masks standing around and sucking the marrow from the center of his bones. And then there was the way everyone kept using that word "harvest." It was as if they were planning to go in, grab the marrow, then toss the remaining chaff onto the compost pile. And any time someone is given general anesthesia, there is a risk.

All these were my own fetid delusions. Andi never revealed to me the slightest hit of nervousness despite my repeated prying about his anxiety level. His little brother's life depended on him. He had given much more of himself to people he hardly knew. There couldn't be a procedure painful enough to prevent him from undergoing it, and this would not be painful at all. The only risk, that of the anesthesia, was minimal, he reassured me.

Three hours after the doctors knocked Andi out, a nurse came into my room with a tray full of intravenous bags full of bone marrow, and hooked the first one up to the IV line.

Now would come the moment of truth, as they introduced this foreign matter into my system. All the earlier tests had shown that Andi's marrow matched mine. But this was not a test. The doctors now monitored me very closely; my skin, my heart rate, my blood pressure. An hour passed and all my indicators remained normal. They increased the flow speed. Two hours later, Andi's marrow was circulating through my blood, slowly working its way into the heart of my skeletal system. I was becoming a new man. ●

MIKE

14 — Surviving the Cure

MODERN MEDICINE and Andi's bone marrow had given me another chance at life. Now my body had to be accommodating enough to accept Andi's marrow while vigilant enough to destroy every other foreign life form that preyed on my vulnerability. To help me walk this fine line, Dr. Kolb kept me sheltered inside L21 from mid-February to mid-April.

We knew early on that this would be the most critical period as my body waged this internal life-or-death battle. Bettina had arranged to take a month off from her job in the Starnberg bank's marketing department. For the next month, she would visit me every morning and afternoon, then spend most evenings at my bedside.

One of our main challenges during this period was to maintain my physical condition. If I succumbed to the sickness and just lay in the bed, I would quickly become frail—exactly when I needed my strength the most. By now I could hardly turn the wheel of my exercise bike. My once-brisk walks around the room, tethered to the ever-present IV tube, traced the same small circle ever more slowly. It didn't help matters that if the tube brushed the floor a nurse would have to immediately sterilize it, lest germs end up in bed with me.

I also had to be obsessive about my personal hygiene. To stave off the threat of infection from outside, I washed thoroughly in the morning and again in the evening. But the hospital could not get the shower filters to work: contaminants kept appearing in the water. So instead of being able to find some comfort in a nice, hot shower, I was reduced to standing in the middle of the bathroom floor, my infusion tube stretched across the room, washing myself down with smelly liquid soap. After sponging the soap across my body, I would rinse myself off, one cupful at a time, with water from the tap. Before long I became too infirm to stand. As the nurses or Bettina washed me, all I could do was slump in a small plastic chair.

Another side effect of the radiation treatment was that my gums and teeth had been severely compromised. To avoid infection from abrasions to my sensitive gums, I wasn't allowed to brush my teeth for three months. At first, I remember thinking that this was a great reprieve from banal routine. How many nights have I wanted to stay in my nice warm bed watching TV and eating a snack rather than getting up to brush. But after about the first week of gargling with medicinal-tasting mouthwash, I had nothing but fond memories of my good old toothbrush.

This critical period in my treatment was also a tedious one. Growing progressively weaker, I spent more and more time just lying in bed, unable to do much of anything. The smallest things grew into intolerable annoyances—even the orderlies, who twice a day cleaned my room and my body. "They barge into my room and start banging all these metal trays around. It's starting to drive me crazy," I remember complaining to Uli one evening. "They use all these nasty-smelling disinfectants and make me get up out of bed all the time." Ever patient, Uli would remind me that they weren't doing this to irritate me, but to help keep me alive. Of course I knew this. But I still resented their intrusions into my little world. The only thing I could do was to clamp my Walkman over my ears as soon as they walked into the room, crank up the volume, and try to ignore them.

Another constant irritant was the battery of drug pumps that hung on the wall on either side of my bed, injecting into my bloodstream calibrated doses of dozens of medicines. After endless nights lying in bed in an otherwise still room, I came to know the sound of each individual pump.

Most of them used a screw mechanism to compress a syringe and inject the drug into the IV flow. Even the smallest air bubble introduced during this process into the IV line could be deadly. It would travel down the tube into my bloodstream and could cut off blood flow to my brain, causing a potentially fatal stroke. To guard against this, each pump had a fail-safe mechanism that detected when fluids being pumped into the IV tube were not flowing continuously. This usually happened a few times over the course of a day. Each time, the mechanism would make a little click that stopped the device from pumping, hesitate a millisecond, then start beeping an alarm. Each time, I would then push the button above my bed and a nurse would come within a minute or two, check for bubbles, clear the alarm, and get the pump going again.

Many were the nights when I would be sound asleep and awake to that little click. It was the small hesitation that followed, not the alarm a moment later, that drove me crazy. Still half asleep, I would press the button, put my head under the blankets, and wait for the nurse to come in and shut off the alarm—knowing that with all the pumps in my room, the whole thing could, and invariably would, happen again any minute.

Considering the amount of stress I was under, I suppose it was only natural for me to be in such a delicate mental state. I had gotten the "cure." Now I had to live with the proverbial eight-hundred-pound gorilla sitting in my hospital room: waiting to see whether my body would accept Andi's bone marrow and start producing blood cells again.

Even with my immune system virtually destroyed by the radiation and chemo, my body was still capable of rejecting the marrow, which it might perceive as an alien life form. This rejection is known as the graft-versus-host (GVH) reaction, and it is dangerous. Not only can GVH quickly destroy transplanted tissues such as bone marrow, organs, and limbs, it can also degenerate into a kind of permanent condition in which the patient must be constantly medicated in order to survive. In extreme cases, GVH can kill the patient outright.

To minimize this risk of GVH, Dr. Ledderose added to my daily drug cocktail an immunosuppressant called Cyclosporin. The tricky part was that since the Cyclosporin further diminished my immune system, it increased the already very serious risk of infection. Ledderose had to be very cautious of the Cyclosporin levels in my blood. Blood samples were now taken every third day—not painlessly through the Hickman, but directly from my veins.

The sign that Kolb and Ledderose looked for during this period, the one change in my body that would lead me safely through the dual risks of rejection and infection, was a rise in my white blood cell count. An increase in this one measurement would mean that my body had accepted Andi's marrow and was using it to produce infection-fighting cells.

Immediately after the transplant my white blood cell count was in the hundreds-per-microliter range. Now the count was supposed to slowly increase. After about three weeks, if my recovery was on track, it would quickly jump to more than one thousand cells per microliter. Once the count reached two thousand, I would be well enough to leave the hospital. But until then, all anyone could really do was to keep the drugs flowing, make sure I was as clean and comfortable as possible—and keep me company. My training team managed these responsibilities flawlessly—until one night in late February.

At this time of year in Germany it gets light in the morning after seven and grows dark by five. Ten hours of light means fourteen hours of dark, a lot of night for a man isolated in a sealed room.

With the doctors, nurses, and orderlies, there were always plenty of people during the day to keep me distracted. In the early evening, Uli, Christine, Reinhard, or Bettina would come to talk or watch TV with me. On most evenings, if Bettina wasn't already in my room, she would soon return to the hospital, check in with whichever member of the support team had been "on duty" that night, and settle herself into a chair by my bed. She and I would chat about my day in the ward and her day in the world, rejoice or fret about my condition, or sometimes just sit quietly until I fell asleep. Around ten or eleven or midnight, Bettina would get up, stretch, and, if I was still awake (which I usually was), lean down and whisper goodnight.

But after she would leave, the night would drag on and on. I came to truly dread these hours. The only thing that made it bearable was that someone had come by to visit and shortened the time I had to face alone.

One morning, Bettina called me to say that she might not be able to make it to the hospital at the usual time. She explained that she was stuck in a business meeting that might run late but would probably make it to the hospital a little after seven that evening.

About noon, she called again and told me that the meeting

would definitely run late—how much so she couldn't yet say.

Neither of us expressed any concern about her not being there at the usual time. Up until then, I had always managed to make it through to morning without any problems—however much I dreaded the prospect of having to do so each night. Of course, I had always had someone there to help pass the evenings.

At five o'clock the next morning I called Bettina. I was completely unhinged, and just kept repeating, "You have to come. You have to come."

When she got to the hospital forty-five minutes later, I was completely unnerved—and angry. I said that her inability to get out of the meeting had been utterly thoughtless. "Look," I said to her, "Don't ever let this happen again. I don't care how you do it, how you manage it, but I don't ever want to be alone again like that for as long as I'm in here. I can't take it."

Bettina looked at me with a combination of sadness and incomprehension. After a moment's consideration, she told me that she hadn't been stuck in a meeting at all. That morning, during her annual OB-GYN visit, her doctor had found a polyp on her ovaries. He didn't want to take any chances, so he immediately sent her to a nearby hospital to have it removed. Once there, she was immediately examined, then told to go to the waiting room...and wait...and wait. It wasn't until late afternoon that the doctors finally had time to squeeze in the surgery. By then, she realized that there was no way she was going to make it to my room and called for the final time. When I asked her why she didn't just tell me the truth, she told me that she hadn't wanted to worry me.

When Bettina finished talking, I apologized contritely. She told me that she didn't understand why I had reacted so harshly. All I could say was that with so many hours without any kind of stimulation—no visitors, no TV (this was before the days of twenty-four-hour cable TV), no music—I had severed the shackles to reality and spiraled down into an hourslong, nearly hallucinogenic, waking nightmare. As I lay there hour after hour, the hope that had sustained me thus far began to leach out of me. I found myself suddenly suspicious of everything the doctors had told me: Maybe my white cell count wasn't improving. Maybe I wasn't going to survive. Maybe I was about to die. At one point it actually seemed like I could feel the life leaking out of me. I feared that any minute now, in this dark, dismal room, I would expire. It was really more than I could bear.

For someone who was used to spending large stretches of time by myself, whether working on my little electronics projects or in front of my Atari creating little spinning planets, that one long night burned into me one realization: I couldn't fight this battle alone.

Ten days after I received the bone marrow transplant, my white blood cell count was rising from one hundred per microliter to around five hundred. Even though the count was low, I had enough white blood cells in me now to heal the sores in my mouth and throat.

Dr. Ledderose told us the count needed to quickly rise to more than one thousand, which they expected to happen within about three weeks of the transplant. But nothing happened. For the next few weeks it continued to fluctuate between five hundred and nine hundred.

A month after the transplant, my blood count hovered where it should have been two weeks earlier. We started to worry that something had gone wrong and that the doctors were afraid to tell us. We asked Kolb and Ledderose more questions. While we got some conflicting explanations, the one we wanted to believe was that my blood count was still within normal parameters—especially with this type of leukemia.

Every day, we waited for the latest blood test results from the lab; every day brought more disappointment. The lab results became the focus of our existence. If my blood count didn't improve soon, I wouldn't survive. There was nothing else we could do but wait. The suspense was excruciating.

Dr. Ledderose was clearly elated one morning when he burst into my room and said that finally, after forty-two days of waiting, my white blood cell count had passed the magic one thousand-per-microliter barrier. I wasn't out of harm's way yet, he said: my white blood cell count was still low. But he said I was on track to quickly reach the fifteen hundred to two thousand cells per microliter mark that signaled a solid recovery. It was time for me to get ready to go home.

A blood count still far below the normal range of four thousand to eight thousand cells per microliter meant that my immune system was still very weak. But as anyone associated with the medical profession knows, hospitals are not necessarily the best places in the world for sick people. They are meeting places where hundreds of people—each with their own dangerous cargo of viruses, microbes, bacteria, and germs—come together to be healed. Given that, Dr. Kolb and Dr. Ledderose thought that the best strategy was to discharge me as soon as feasible. I could pursue my recovery from home.

Leaving the hospital after all that I had been through, however, was not simply a matter of getting out of bed, getting dressed, and walking out the door. There were two problems. For the past three months, I had received every breakfast, lunch, and dinner through an IV tube. Before I could leave, I would need to learn to eat solid food again. At the same time, I would need to regain my physical strength.

The effect of going so long without eating in the traditional sense was that I didn't feel hungry anymore. We tend to think that if we stop consuming food, we experience hunger. But there is something very elegant, if completely unnatural, about getting nutrition through an IV tube. You're never hungry because you constantly receive a small trickle of nutrition straight into your veins. Bowel movements become a rarity. Most people on IV still go to the bathroom, only because much of what is in our waste is dead blood cells. But I, having been bombarded with X-rays and chemotherapy, still didn't have many extra blood cells, new or old, to eliminate.

For someone going off what amounted to a three-month fast, I thought that I might start by eating light foods such as salads and fresh fruit. But these foods contained fungal spores. Things like dried cereal, oatmeal, and pasta were not allowed because they were too hard for me to digest. With all these restrictions, my first "real" meal in three months consisted of rusk bread, or Zwieback, the slightly sweetened toast given to babies, and tea.

Even on a beginner's diet that soon progressed all the way to canned baby food, I started to experience digestive problems. Immediately after starting on these solid foods, I started throwing up again—so much so that Dr. Kolb and Dr. Ledderose decided to perform an endoscopy.

The next morning as I lay sedated in my bed, Dr. Ledderose inserted into my throat a small surgical tube with a camera mounted on the end. He slowly forced it down my esophagus and into my stomach, and began scanning the lining for signs of ulcer or some other possible cause for the vomiting.

Twenty-four hours later, when Bettina had dropped by for a visit, Dr. Ledderose came up and tapped lightly on the airlock window. He gestured for Bettina to come outside. Ledderose told her then that he hadn't found anything in the endoscopy images to explain the nausea. "We have an idea of what's causing it," he told her. "But, given, what Mike has been through, we don't want to tell him what it is."

Bettina must have blanched because Dr. Ledderose quickly said, "Wait, I didn't say that right. I don't mean that there is some terrible cause. I mean there is no cause at all. It is psychosomatic. There is nothing wrong with him."

Ledderose asked Bettina not to tell me that my own mind was the only thing keeping me in the hospital now. But she knew me well enough to know as soon as I understood the only thing keeping me in this god-forsaken room was my inability to keep food down, I would get over it.

This entire episode was frustrating to us all because I had been so close to getting out. We knew it would be better for me to be discharged as soon as possible. But there was no way the doctors could let me leave when I wasn't able to eat. It was turning out to be as hard to get out of that room as it had been to get in.

At one point, Bettina privately asked Dr. Ledderose if I might better work on my eating problem at home. "You don't understand how serious this is," answered the doctor. "We have to be sure that when he leaves the hospital he doesn't die from malnutrition. At the rate he's going, that is a distinct possibility."

Bettina was right in following her instincts and telling me about the nausea. Three days after she told me, my vomiting ceased.

Even before this milestone, I had begun the work of recovering my physical strength. Despite our best efforts over the previous three months, I had been reduced from multisport athlete to shuffling apparition. As with my dietary journey, my physical reconditioning program began with similar baby steps out the door of my isolation room and down the hall.

Although I was still inside the Station L21 cocoon, I had to don protective gear to leave my room. At first, simply putting on the hospital scrubs, the coat, the face mask, and clogs wore me out. But before long I was huffing and puffing up and down the corridor, getting my first chance to say hello to people outside of my medical and support teams.

At first, I marked my progress by seeing how many doorways I could pass as I walked, bent forward like someone bucking a strong headwind. After a couple weeks, I graduated to walking the halls outside of L21. Then one day Dr. Ledderose came into my room and, smiling broadly at his prize patient, said "Okay. I think you're ready for the real world now. How about taking a walk outside?"

I had watched through my window as the seasons passed from winter to spring. But the change in seasons hadn't mattered much. Nor had politics or sports scores. Nothing had mattered but my recovery. I had been caged up so long that I wondered if I could face the immense world beyond the leukemia ward. Would I cower at the doorway like a mouse or go bolting off into the bushes like a jackrabbit?

Before that question could be answered, we first had to assemble an appropriate outfit—my coming-out apparel, as it were. The medical team knew that exposure to sunlight could trigger the growth of more leukemic cells. For this and subsequent forays into nature, I would need some serious protection.

Finally getting to play a role, however small, in her son's recovery, my mother searched frantically through all the clothes in her three men's wardrobes to come up with the perfect apparel. Looking a bit like a field worker in my father's long baggy khakis, my own old plaid shirt, and a floppy brimmed gardening hat of Andi's, I sallied forth for the first time in months out into the fresh air.

My first words upon leaving the hospital for my inaugural walk were not profound. "Wow! It's cold outside here," I exclaimed to no one in particular. I was no longer just observing the world. I was a part of it. It was now mid-April, 1991. I had been isolated from the world for eleven and half weeks. I was ready to leave the hospital and rejoin the human race.

After just the third or fourth walk it seemed perfectly natural to be outside again. With my faith restored that I could leave my little cocoon and still survive, and with my appetite quickly returning, I started to believe that it might be possible for my life to return to normal in other ways as well.

The final step was for Dr. Ledderose to remove the Hickman catheter. After administering a small dose of local anesthetic, Dr. Ledderose pulled the tube out and stuck a little bandage on my hairless chest. At that instant, I felt like a newborn baby: disconnected from my umbilical cord, weak, fragile, squinting at the light—but determined to learn to live. Again.

the duathlon

Bumpy Re-entry

BY MID-MORNING ON APRIL 20, the sun had enough strength to cut between the billowing cumulus clouds and brighten the buds on my mother's apple trees. It was the Saturday before Mike would be discharged from the hospital, and Uli was coming over to help me get our apartment ready. I was upstairs cleaning when I heard Uli pull her father's station wagon up the gravel driveway. As she walked toward the front door, she stopped to chat with my father, who was on his hands and knees clearing wet leaves from an onion bed.

All our windows were open, with a light breeze blowing the curtains and the first flies of spring wandering between rooms. I called down to Uli from a bedroom window and she headed up the stairs. Her blue eyes sparkled as she looked up. She was as excited as I was that Mike would soon be home again.

Dressed in old jeans and a T-shirt, with shoulder-length auburn hair pulled back under a bandana, Uli looked tanned, fit, and healthy. As she ran up the stairs, I was just putting the last of the knickknacks into boxes. I had already packed up all the books to transfer to the cellar. I had given all of our house plants to my mother and a few to friends.

My goal was to remove anything from our house that could harbor dust or germs. Literally everything, of course, carried dust, so Uli helped me figure out which things constituted an acceptable level of risk. She carried boxes to the basement, then rolled up the rugs and put them in her car.

When we were finished, our once homey apartment looked disconcertingly like Mike's hospital room.

Mike came home the following Thursday afternoon. Thumbtacked to the front of the house was a sign that Andi, who was a terrific artist, had mailed me. It was a big, hand-painted white banner with "Herzlich Willkommen, Mike" in the center in Bavarian light blue, surrounded by a delicate ellipse of Andi's watercolor depictions of the flowers he worked with every day.

Mike's parents, Uli and her boyfriend, and a gathering of our friends were standing around in the front yard when we drove up. Everyone knew that we weren't going to pop open a bottle of champagne (as much as Mike would have loved it), and there wouldn't be any hors d'oeuvres.

Mike climbed slowly out of the car and started for the front door. I could see how much everyone wanted to give him a big hug and a kiss—and how much he needed it. But at this point those things represented risk, not affection. Everyone simply offered him their best wishes and left us alone, as they would for many months ahead.

At first, we tried to return to some measure of normality. But it was difficult. Home again, but without the same dedicated support group, unable to socialize for fear of catching even a small cold, and without the stamina to return to work, Mike became short-tempered and listless.

When I went back to work again the following week, Mike was spending entire days without seeing anyone at all. After that one evening when I had my operation, we should have known that it wasn't good for him to be alone too much. But we were so glad he was home and on the road to recovery that we didn't pay much attention to his changing moods.

Around this time I was offered the job at Clarins, and finally left the Starnberg bank. That meant more of a commute and, as with all new jobs, more late nights.

Within a month of having Mike home again, we decided we needed our own home and put a down payment on a two-bedroom condominium less than a mile from my parents' home. Shortly thereafter, I decided to go back to school. Mike had an advanced degree while I had what amounted to a degree from a junior college. Once I started working for Clarins, it became clear to me that if I wanted to get anywhere in the world of business—and I did—then I would need more education. So in the fall of 1991 I began taking classes at night at the Bavarian Academy of Marketing Communications. Maybe the timing wasn't perfect, but after focusing on Mike for so long I felt the time had come for me to pay some attention to my own needs.

With all this time on his hands, Mike was becoming increasingly irritable. We decided that we probably disbanded the Bone Marrow Olympics Training Team too precipitously, and asked everyone if they would be willing to reform a "lite" version of the team. Karin, Reini, and Christine now made renewed efforts to drop by during the day to visit Mike. And Uli came by every day or at least called him on the phone.

Even though I was meeting people at night school, about six months after Mike's discharge I had started feeling depressed, too. It seemed like none of our friends ever dropped by to say hello. We didn't understand that they were avoiding us because they didn't know how to act around us. Should they ask about the illness? About the treatment? How Mike felt now? Or should they try to avoid the subject entirely and pretend nothing ever happened? No one knew what to do, how to act, what to say.

We wanted them to know that, yes, we had been through a lot, but were the same people we were before. We wanted them to understand that they could ask either of us anything about the treatment or the illness. If we didn't want to tell them something, we wouldn't. But they didn't need to avoid it. We knew that many cared deeply about what had happened. And we imagined that many people were simply very curious about the whole thing. We wanted them to feel free to ask about anything.

The problem was that we hadn't told anyone any of this. They were completely in the dark, afraid of offending us, afraid of bringing up topics that we wanted to avoid, afraid of seeming overly curious or insensitive. So naturally, a wall had been erected between us and them.

Maybe it was because of the approach of the Christmas season that Mike and I finally decided to do something. We wanted to reconnect with our friends so we spent many evening explaining to them our feelings about discussing Mike's disease. By and large, they appreciated our willingness to reach out to them in this way. Barriers to communication slowly fell, and we were able to spend the holidays feeling once again like we belonged to a community.

We also had to learn to take it very seriously every time Mike got a runny nose or sore throat, anytime he felt particularly weak or didn't feel hungry or had a small headache. For normal patients, doctors would respond to these complaints with the usual "take two aspirin and call me in the morning." For Mike, though, every little infection, however innocuous it seemed, was still potentially fatal.

It is the first year following bone marrow transplant, during which time the immune system is slowly rebuilding itself, that the patient faces the highest risk of death. For the first two months after his discharge, Mike had to go back to the leukemia ward three times a week for an exam and blood tests.

As his recovery progressed, Dr. Ledderose reduced the visits to just once a week, then once every two weeks, until he was eventually going in just once every three months—then only for the blood tests.

In addition to these scheduled visits, we raced those nineteen minutes to the Universitätsklinik Grosshadern four times over the next couple of years—fearing each time that a cold or flu might put Mike's life in danger. Each time, he was treated with huge doses of antibiotics, instructed to keep the doctors informed of any change in his condition, and sent home.

On one such ordinary visit in October of 1993, the blood test showed an abnormally high white blood cell count. Instead of the normal four thousand to eight thousand per microliter, Mike's had shot back up to fifty thousand. It wasn't the two hundred thousand that first led to the CML diagnosis. But it was high enough. The leukemia was back.

Relapse

AT FIRST I THOUGHT I had pretty much run out of options. Sure, I could go back on the hydroxyurea cocktail or even try the allopathic transplant using my own marrow. But neither of those alternatives would give me more than a few years of life. I was only thirty years old. I wanted more.

Only after a long series of discussions did Dr. Kolb and Dr. Ledderose tell us that a second allogeneic bone marrow transplant was possible. They had held back, they said, because a second transplant meant that we would have to start from scratch and repeat the entire radiation therapy and chemotherapy. A second transplant had been tried only in rare cases and had seldom succeeded.

Because the first attempt had failed here in Germany, Bettina and I thought about doing the second transplant somewhere else, maybe in a different hospital in Europe. We even entertained the idea again of having the procedure done in the Seattle hospital where José Carreras was treated in 1988.

Then a leading physician from another German hospital told us that going to a foreign hospital wouldn't really make much of a difference: German physicians had caught up with their American counterparts. If we did decide to try it again overseas, we would have to come up with the $400,000 to cover the cost of care. Three months after I left the hospital in April 1991, I had returned to my previous job as a contract programmer at AKM, working with the latest C++ programming language. By that fall I had become a full-time employee. But even with our combined incomes there was no way Bettina and I would ever be able to raise that kind of money. Even if we succeeded in begging, borrowing, or stealing it, I knew I would never be able to go through another transplant. It was too hard.

These first weeks following the news of my relapse devastated Bettina and me, our families, and our friends—probably more so than when I was first diagnosed. Back then, we figured that since I wasn't the first person on the planet to get this form of cancer, there would surely be a cure. Now it looked like our only option was to come up with hundreds of thousands of dollars to pay for a second bone marrow transplant that, even if performed in Seattle, held out little hope—and which, in any case, I doubted I could survive. Bettina and I, thinking that I had run out of options, cried a lot at this point,

Then one day, Dr. Kolb and Dr. Ledderose asked us to come talk to them at the hospital. Sitting in Dr. Kolb's office, they told us that in the past three years they had been working on a new form of leukemia treatment. They were calling it donor leukocyte infusion (DLI) because it involved the transplant not of entire bone marrow, but of just the donor's white blood cells, or leukocytes. The idea was that rather than destroying a patient's immune system, it might work better to buttress it by injecting healthy white blood cells from a donor. Unlike a complete bone marrow transplant, DLI did not involve radiation or chemotherapy.

They had hesitated to raise this option earlier because if I decided to try the donor leukocyte injection, I would be doing so as a virtual guinea pig. Dr. Kolb said that the DLI patients who had already received the treatment were responding well—but they had tried it on just two patients, hardly enough to make any conclusions about its efficacy. We had come to trust these men so much that it seemed like the most credible alternative—especially if it meant that I wouldn't have to face another round of preconditioning.

Four weeks after my new diagnosis and two and half years since I thought I had left it for good, I was back in Station L21. On October 18, 1993, Andi arrived once again from Switzerland, ready to help in my recovery. All Dr. Ledderose had to do this time was sit Andi down in a chair, stick a needle in his left arm, draw the blood out, pass it through a centrifuge to remove the leukocytes, then run it back into his right arm: no anesthesia, no poking holes in his pelvis. The whole process took about three hours, and the only thing Andi noticed was that the blood coming back into his arm was colder than when it left.

Once Ledderose centrifuged the white cells out of Andi's blood, he transfused them into me. He also started me up again on interferon alpha injections. He and Dr. Kolb were convinced that the addition of donor leukocytes, together with the interferon, would initiate a complex process that would destroy the leukemic cells that were once again multiplying wantonly in my bone marrow.

At first, all went well. But before long I started feeling the effects of the interferon alpha, to which my body had never really been able to adjust. I felt sick all the time, with a constant headache that made it hard for me to concentrate on anything. By November, I stopped working and spent most of the time lying on the couch, depressed again, tired, and watching a lot of TV.

Because I was trying a new treatment modality, the two doctors wanted me to report frequently to the hospital in the months following the donor leukocyte injection. One of the possible complications of the DLI (similar to that of a full transplant) is that the donor leukocytes, designed as they are to attack foreign life forms, can begin to attack not just leukemic cells but the patient's own bone marrow—which would manifest as a drop in the white blood cell count. Each time I came to the hospital, Dr. Ledderose would use a screwdriver-like tool to take a small pelvic bone marrow sample from me. By analyzing the composition of the marrow, he and Dr. Kolb could watch for the presence of overly aggressive leukocytes.

Sure enough, by January 1994 my white blood cell count was sinking fast—way too fast. By the middle of the month, it had dropped from a pre-DLI high of fifty thousand per microliter to less than fourteen hundred. It had sounded great in theory. But Andi's leukocytes had turned on me and were destroying my bone marrow.

Back into the hospital I went. It didn't help matters that I ended up in the very same room I had vacated in April, 1991. After more than three years of aggressively fighting this chronic myeloid leukemia, I was right where I started. No, that's not true. I was—we were—exhausted, spent, worn down, and worn out. Anything we tried now would be out of sheer desperation.

Given the failure of the donor leukocyte infusion, Drs. Kolb and Ledderose told me that the next option was to try an even newer, even more experimental treatment: stem cell transplant. It would mean another long stay in the hospital—perhaps as much as two months.

Dr. Ledderose assured me that it wouldn't be painful and I wouldn't be on any kind of sedating drugs. I would feel as healthy as

I did then, which wasn't too bad. And I could read, write, and watch TV just like I was staying in a hotel room. I could even bring in some work if I wanted to.

For the first time since Christmas Eve, 1989, I began to contemplate not surviving the leukemia after all. The more I thought about my mortality, the more I wanted to leave a mark on the world. These feelings were heightened one day when Bettina was visiting me. Uli came to the hospital and stood outside my window holding a little bundle in her arms: my one-week-old nephew, Frederik. Knowing we could never have children of our own, Bettina and I stood together in this little antiseptic room, looking out, and crying in both joy and sorrow.

Thanks to the initial radiation treatment and chemotherapy and all of those other feckless cures, there would be no little Michael Juniors running around our house. I wasn't a writer capable of brilliantly summing up his life, or an artist like Andi who, moved by the vision of his own mortality, might paint his final masterpiece. I was a thirty-year-old software programmer who could slip into the acute phase of leukemia at any moment and be dead in six months. If I was going to create a legacy, I'd have to do it by sticking to what I knew best.

I began to review my short career as a programmer. I realized that what had always excited me most was the idea of creating a perfect computer interface. My friends and I at the technical university in Munich had dreamed of creating such an interface. That was what had prompted us to create the Atari Computer Club.

Now all I had to do was survive long enough to create it.

The coming hospital stay metamorphosed from a prison stay to a chance to create my legacy—if, that is, they let me bring my computer into my isolation room. ▪

17 — Mind Man

THE SMALL GRAY METAL TABLE that one of the orderlies had disinfected for me stood against the wall at the foot of my bed. He had also rummaged up a molded plastic chair and a desk lamp. Sitting at my impromptu work station in my hospital scrubs, I could look out the picture window three paces to my left. Five paces to my right was the door to the airlock. It was 10:17 a.m. on Sunday, January 11, 1994, according to the calendar window on the computer sitting there in front of me.

Tomorrow I would begin my stem cell therapy. Found in the highest concentrations inside the bone marrow, stem cells create all the different parts of blood: the red cells, white cells, platelets, and other factors. By introducing compatible stem cells into a CML patient's blood stream, these healthy cells would create "good" blood faster than the marrow would produce "bad" blood. Or so goes the theory behind stem cell therapy.

In the late 1980s, medical researchers discovered a naturally occurring hormone that stimulates the production of infection-fighting white blood cells. This so-called granulocyte colony stimulating factor was also found to increase the supply of stem cells in the blood. No longer would doctors need to puncture a donor's pelvic bones to get the quantity of stem cells required. Five days before the scheduled stem-cell transplant, Dr. Ledderose started Andi on this stimulating factor. By the time of the transfusion, there was more than a one-hundred-fold increase in the number of stem cells in Andi's blood. On January 12, 1994, Dr. Ledderose installed a Hickman catheter in my chest and Andi's blood began to flow in my veins once again.

Every day now I would face the usual interruptions by orderlies, the blood tests, the doctor visits. But this time I would have all the time in the world to program. Having my meals provided, having someone else do the dishes, and having my own room took on a new luster.

I felt so buoyed by the prospect of creating the perfect graphic interface that I had returned to the leukemia ward with perhaps more optimism than I had a right to feel. I wanted to believe this time that, even if the stem cell transplant failed, something good might come out of this whole mess. This time, instead of passing the hours lying in bed listening to CDs and watching TV, I would create my precious little gift to the world.

I had the time. I had the place. Now all I needed was the right idea. Like a lost hiker climbing tree after tree to find his way through dense woods, I grappled with all the ideas I had ever mentally filed away. Each one had its moment in my little room, as I toyed with various visions of the path ahead. Then suddenly it came to me.

Ever since I was first introduced to it a few years earlier, I had made mind mapping a part of my work processes—but I had always struggled with it. Not being much of an artist, I found it hard to follow the "rules" of mind mapping regarding the use of colors, hand-drawn images, and other visual cues. I couldn't draw to save my life, and it seemed ridiculously unprofessional to walk into a meeting with a set of colored pens in hand to create a map. But what about a software program that provided the maps, complete with colors and symbols, on a computer?

I didn't have the faintest clue about how to begin. I just had this image of a mind map and the notion that, somehow, I should be able to get that image into the computer.

I knew that there needed to be a central title that would help focus the information and ideas entered into the map. Users would also need to be able to add branches off the main title, sub-branches off those branches, and so on, to create as many layers as necessary to capture everything they needed. Could I design my mind-mapping software to follow the sequence I followed every time I built a map by hand?

I enjoyed about three weeks of solid programming time in my isolation room. Then one morning Dr. Ledderose came in to tell me that my medical team was getting cold feet. My blood values hadn't returned to normal following the stem-cell transplant. Not only was my white blood cell count low, but I was no longer producing red blood cells or platelets. I was becoming anemic. I started receiving whole blood transfusions every other day. The transfusions helped stabilize my situation, but the body can exist on borrowed cells for only so long. After a month or so of these transfusions, my body would start to reject this borrowed blood.

"Look," he said, "we aren't going to rely on the stem cells alone any more. It's a good theory, and we've done a lot of research on it. But it just doesn't seem to work for you. And if we continue on this course of treatment and your body starts to reject your brother's blood, we will have one treatment option left: another second bone marrow transplant. If that doesn't work—and there is a good chance that it won't, we will be out of options. You won't survive."

He said that while we would need to attempt another marrow transfusion, it would be in a gentler form. Because my system was now familiar with Andi's bone marrow, there was no need for another round of radiation and chemotherapy to suppress my body's natural reaction to reject foreign cells. It was true that my marrow wasn't pro-ducing enough blood parts because it was being attacked by my brother's leukocytes. But this was a relatively mild reaction that could be controlled with immunosuppressant drugs.

That night I had to call Andi and ask him to come down for the fourth time: I needed his marrow again. When he arrived the next afternoon, he came directly into my room and sat down beside my bed. As was his way, it took him a few moments to gather his thoughts.

"Mike," he finally said, "I want to make sure you understand that you don't ever have to worry about asking me to do this—any of this. You're my brother and I will do anything you need me to do to help you beat this. I am here to help."

As we were talking, Dr. Ledderose entered the room to say hello to Andi. I accused Dr. Ledderose of being a hopeless roman-tic for scheduling my second bone marrow transplant exactly three years to the day after the first one: on Valentine's Day. He laughed and said it had just worked out that way by chance. I took that as a good sign.

The next morning, Andi was wheeled into a surgical room and given general anesthesia. Dr. Ledderose used the same multiple puncture method he had used before to remove the necessary liter and a half of Andi's bone marrow. Later that day I received my second bone marrow transplant.

Two days later, my blood values started to improve. This was a startling development because it happened far too soon to have been the result of the marrow transplant. The doctors concluded that the stem-cell transplant must have worked after all. It had just taken longer than they were comfortable with. The second bone marrow transplant might not have been necessary after all, but there was no way of knowing for sure. To be very safe this time, I stayed in the isolation room and on immunosuppressants for another six weeks.

To my sheer delight, I found that this trip to L21 couldn't have been more different from my first—mostly because there was no radiation or chemotherapy. I never felt nauseous. My hair never fell out. And, to her great relief, my mother could finally come to the hospital and dote on her son—bringing me the home-cooked meals I craved: chicken with rice, filet mignon, spaetzle, and wiener schnitzel. I could also receive more visitors this time—not just the members of my support team, but anyone who wanted to drop by. I could get all the exercise I wanted. And I could work. The only thing I couldn't do was leave the leukemia ward. Were it not for that and the fact that everyone who came to see me was wearing identical blue hospital scrubs and face masks, I could have passed for just another geek holed up in some apartment writing the next great piece of code.

Only later did I learn that the other doctors and nurses thought I was an odd patient: while most patients were quietly lying in bed reading or watching TV, I was hunched over my PC for five or six hours a day, creating something called MindMan. Dr. Kolb came in one day to see what I had been working on so intently. He tried to make some joke about how I should consider doing something practical with my life, and left muttering something about how odd it all looked.

Because I didn't have any eating problems this time, I was discharged as soon as my blood values returned to normal. As before, one of the last steps was to remove the Hickman from my chest—a simple procedure, like removing a syringe from a vein, that had gone the last time without a hitch.

This time though, after Dr. Ledderose removed the catheter, a bubbling sound came from my chest and a strange feeling rippled throughout my body. It felt like an electric shock and nearly caused me to faint. Dr. Ledderose put his palm on my chest and pressed down firmly. When he did this, he realized that air from my lungs was being expelled directly into the room.

During this time, Bettina had been standing on the other side of the treatment room window, my street clothes in hand, calmly waiting to drive me home. Instead, she saw the doctor and two nurses panic and strap an oxygen mask on my face. One of the nurses noticed Bettina growing agitated on the other side of the window and intercepted her before she could come into the room. Between the "oops," the very disturbing sensation I was feeling, the oxygen mask, and the nurse's sudden departure, I thought for a few seconds that it was all over this time, but that Dr. Ledderose just wasn't going to tell me so.

It turned out that six weeks earlier when he had inserted the Hickman, he had nicked my lung. All this time, the catheter had blocked the hole. But as soon as he removed the tube, the hole opened up. While not life-threatening, it frightened the wits out of me, Bettina, the nurses and, most of all, Dr. Ledderose.

For months afterward, I often woke up in the middle of the night in a cold sweat, overwhelmed by the sensation that the hole had opened back up again. I would have to lie there very still, with my hand on my chest, listening to each breath, until I was sure that I could not hear that awful bubbling sound.

Other than this, my recovery proceeded on track—and I had made tremendous gains in creating the first working version of the mind-mapping program. My original motivation—to leave a legacy— had been replaced by the urge to complete what Bettina and I had come to think was a promising piece of software.

In retrospect, though, MindMan was still more than that. I felt as if the software had saved me. If I hadn't had this project to develop while I was in the hospital, the second relapse, the apparent failure of the DLI, the anemia, and the fear that I had run out of options might have done me in.

Many programmers get halfway through a project and move on to something else. I couldn't let something that had meant so much to me end up as just another forgotten file on a discarded computer in my attic. Could I finish the program, get it out in the marketplace, and see if anyone liked it? ▪

MIKE

More Champagne, Please

SOON AFTER MIKE WAS DISCHARGED from the hospital this time, he left AKM and took a programming job at PC Plus, working after hours to finish up MindMan 1.0. Still at Clarins, I took on the task of getting it in front of potential users, using the copying machine at work to create our first brochures. We knew nothing about selling software. After searching through computer magazines, we learned about software resellers, businesses that serve as a kind of a hub to help software vendors reach end users. We were looking for small resellers that had personal relationships with corporate purchasers, distribution channels to get products to customers, and newsletters to inform customers of new and exciting products on the market. We wrote letters to the four biggest resellers in Germany and asked them if they might be interested in selling mind-mapping software.

Although we had thought that mind mapping was fairly well known, we didn't know if anyone would see the need for mapping software. So when Gerd Zoettlein, who owned the reseller PD-Profi Zoettlein, called back in May 1994, Mike launched into an explanation of the basic concept. Gerd, cutting him off, said, "Yeah, yeah, yeah, I know all about it. I also know the companies that want to have it."

Gerd was already selling another mapping program we had heard rumors about. He was interested in MindMan because we had created the interface in German. VisiMap, the competitor, was available only in English. Gerd also liked that we had created a tool for the business environment. VisiMap seemed better suited for individual users as a kind of creativity tool.

By now, our MindMan had become fairly sophisticated. We had shown it to only a small group of friends. But they were all impressed by the way you could open up a new map, type a title into the oval shape that appeared in the center of the screen, then use the Enter key to create branches radiating out from the center. On each branch, you could type any number of words to represent an idea, a stage in a process, or a task to be accomplished. To each branch, you could insert sub-branches, breaking down larger tasks into smaller ones, or a broad idea into its component parts. At any stage, you could hyperlink these branches to supporting documents. Once you put all your ideas down, you could then drag and drop the branches and sub-branches to put them into a logical sequence. Unlike traditional outlining or list-making software, people who would use MindMan wouldn't get bogged down trying to figure out what came first or next: they would be able to capture all their ideas on the screen first, and organize them later. Most of the people we showed it to agreed that something about the display made it easier to work—it actually made work fun.

We started working with PD-Profi Zoettlein in June, with the grand ambition of selling ten licenses by the end of the year. After the initial excitement of knowing that someone out there was actually going around marketing our new software, we waited for our first sale. A few days went by with no word. "Well, it'll probably take a few months until we hear back from him," Mike said one day. "He'll need to introduce MindMan into his channels and get it placed on shareware CDs. It'll just take some time, that's all." And so we waited.

In the first week of July, Gerd called and announced that he had sold the very first MindMan license to one of those early adopters who was interested in seeing what this "visual thinking" software was all about. A check, albeit a small one, was winging its way to us as we spoke. When it arrived, Mike and I treated ourselves to a fancy seafood dinner at one of the restaurants that looked out on Lake Starnberg. Over glasses of champagne, we watched the lights dance on the water and decided that every time we sold another license, we would have another lavish repast "on the company."

Two weeks later, PD-Profi Zoettlein sold another license—and out we went again. This went on for a few more sales until we realized that we couldn't keep this up. Gerd was selling so many licenses that we would soon be dining out every night. Why put all this money in the pockets of restaurant owners, we thought? Let's build our own business.

By the end of 1994, thanks in part to our first review in a German software magazine, *WIN*, we had sold not ten licenses—but more than four hundred. And we sold them all to different kinds of companies. It wasn't all software developers or project managers or business consultants. We were a kind of "mirror ware": whatever people saw in the software—the promise of an improved ability to right reports, take notes, plan projects, brainstorm a new product or prepare a presentation—MindMan reflected that functionality.

Mike was still on medication, mostly immunosuppresants to help his body accept the bone marrow and antibiotics to ward off infection. As a result, we weren't socializing much. We needed to avoid all the little flus and colds that were a nuisance to others but dangerous to Mike. Instead, we spent most of our nights and weekends working on MindMan.

On Gerd's advice, we got our first CompuServe email account. Even at twenty-four hundred baud per second, it was a thrill to come home in the evening, bring up our email, and communicate with MindMan customers.

Christmas 1994 came and went. Our friends left for ski trips to the Alps and holidays across Europe. We stayed in our apartment most of the time, responding to customers, answering their questions about how to perform certain tasks, and listening to their suggestions on how to improve the software.

At first, it was difficult to hear people criticize a product that had come to mean so much to us. But at the same time it made us realize that MindMan was a living thing that needed to grow and change, just like a person. It soon became obvious to us that we needed to create a second release.

No sooner had we begun to plan version 2.0 than, in the spring of 1995, Mike began having chest pains again. The doctors couldn't figure out what caused it, and it went away after just a few days. But it reminded us that Mike was not finished with the leukemia. He needed to slow down.

Minimizing stress was key to avoiding another relapse, so Mike told his supervisor at PC Plus that he would have to scale down to four days a week. It meant a hit to our income. But on the bright side,

Mike now had three days a week to do what continued to be the best therapy he had found: working on MindMan.

Sometimes when I feel overwhelmed by the responsibility of running a business, I think back to these very first days of our company. We were just a young couple riding the excitement of what was born as a form of therapy but had taken on a life of its own. We didn't mean to start a business, but here we were.

Our first steps were tentative. We worked on the software at night, on weekends, and during vacations. We got the email account. And we turned one of the bedrooms in our Percha condominium into an office.

After all we had been through it was surprisingly pleasant for the two of us to just work quietly in this featureless room for hours on end. I sat on one side of a round table writing the first Help file and building our first accounting system. Mike sat across from me doing the programming. We had plenty of customer support calls and emails to answer. Now we also had a new release to build.

We began to do some rudimentary marketing. We weren't able to simply go out and purchase email addresses like you can today. Nor did we have the money to go to trade shows or send out flyers. Our public-relations work consisted of reading magazines and wondering how to get in touch with the reporters. When we got hold of a magazine that had a list of trainers at the back, we were in heaven. I remember putting each and every one of those addresses in my PC by hand. I had my first direct-mail database!

In the summer of 1995, we received an email from a man in New York named Marty Fox, who told us that he could help us build a Web site and host it for $99 a month. Mike and I signed up and started designing the site. It was up and running in a month. We started getting orders almost immediately—and from around the world. Between the reseller activity and Web orders, we were soon in the position of having to reinvest profits or lose them in taxes.

In addition to the Web site, we managed to find other ways to spend money: creating our first flyer and accumulating computer and office equipment.

Within two years after Mike's relapse, we had made great strides toward building a business. We had customers, an accounting system, marketing activities, a Web site with an online store, software to maintain, and service packs to develop.

As we built a network of small resellers, we received our first introduction to contract negotiations. Dealing with businesspeople much more savvy than us and often communicating in languages other than our native German, we had to resolve complicated issues such as price increases, who would pay for shipping, and how to handle customer problems. Nothing Mike and I had ever done before really prepared us for these kinds of things. We were learning how to run our business day by day, one challenge at a time.

Between Mike's health problems and starting a business, we hadn't taken a real vacation since our honeymoon in 1988—seven years earlier. With our resellers in place to manage customer orders and questions for a few weeks, we decided that the summer of 1995 would be a great time to travel to the far-off lands of Canada and Hawaii.

It was to be our last vacation during which we didn't feel the need to constantly check email (which was a good thing, because at this time it was virtually impossible to do so remotely). Nor were we so enmeshed in our business that we couldn't mentally detach ourselves from it. After everything that had happened in the past five years, we felt as though we had earned the right to an utterly relaxing break. Not that we could relax enough to actually take that break. We wore ourselves out snorkeling, parasailing, swimming, and hiking. We went island hopping and helicopter touring and sailed on catamarans into the tropical sun. After ten days, we were exhausted, but pleasantly so.

Upon our return to Starnberg, one of my first tasks was to create invoices for the sales made while we were drinking Mai Tais and wiggling our toes in the water. We were dumfounded to discover that after being gone four weeks we had earned nearly $6,000! It wasn't a fortune. But for two people who had always earned their living one paycheck at a time, it was very odd to make so much money "doing nothing."

Before we knew it, the business had grown so much that getting away for long became impossible. When we did escape, we spent far too many days at Internet cafés in the Alps or at the beach. Vacations would never again be as carefree or as email-free as that first trip to Hawaii. ▪

BETTINA

Black Sun

TWELVE MEN, TWO TEAMS OF SIX, milled anxiously around computer monitors set up inside two cavernous rooms at a converted Munich furniture warehouse. It was ten o'clock on a fall night in 1995. They had been working toward this moment for six months.

About to appear on their screens, each team hoped, was a simple gray sphere representing the actions of a mouse operated by the team in the other room. This would be the birth, they were convinced, of a new era in computing.

The men were giddy with anticipation, making sporadic hooting noises that echoed in the empty building. One of them, a stout raven-haired programmer named Peter, began a countdown, and they all joined in. At zero, two other programmers, Robert and Thilo, each sitting before computers in their respective rooms, simultaneously launched the application the team had been working on since the summer of 1993.

Nothing happened. Both screens were blank. The air hissed out of both rooms. On the men's faces reflected only the LCD glow of an expectant monitor.

Then in the front room nearest the entrance, one of the senior developers, Kristof, leaned forward a little and stared at the screen. After a moment's hesitation, he placed the tip of his index finger on the screen, turned to the man next to him, and asked, "Is that it?"

The room grew quiet. A few more men peered intently. "No," one of them muttered, "it's only a spot of dirt."

Others weren't so sure. They huddled around the screen—their faces inches apart. Was this tiny speck the avatar they were hoping for, the culmination of months of intense programming—or just a bit of dust?

Suddenly, Kristof shouted out, telling the team in the back room to move the mouse around. Yes, it looked to Kristof's team that a little dot on the screen was moving. But it was hard to tell.

Kristof leaped up from his seat, ran across the hall to the back room, and began madly raking the mouse toward him across the mouse pad.

As the men in the front room watched in rapt attention, the dot began to grow. After a few seconds it was the size of a pea. As though a cork had just popped out of a bottle, the men burst into shouts and guffaws. They had created a way for one computer user's movements within the 3D-space of the Internet to dance across another networked computer: the avatar had arrived.

Everyone in the back room except Kristof dashed up the hall. Before them on the screen was a sphere the size of a grape. Then it became as big as a golf ball. Then a squash ball. As a perfectly formed black sphere the size of a tennis ball came to rest in the foreground of the monitor in the second room, a wild cheer erupted. Kristof finally came over from the other room and everyone began slapping each other on the back.

These men, most of whom I knew from college, had formed a company called Blaxxun. I envied them.

While Bettina and I had been busily growing our little company one sale at a time, these men had gathered a ton of money to start Blaxxun (originally called Black Sun until Sun Microsystems accused them of trademark infringement. In response, Blaxxun had changed its name—but just barely.)

From the outset, Blaxxun received its operating capital not from sales but from investors. Venture capital investment was virtually unknown in Germany at this time; it was decidedly un-German to give someone money to build a company that, like Blaxxun, had neither real products nor real customers.

At this time, Blaxxun was one of the many companies—but one of the few in Germany—pushing Internet avatars. George Lucas's LucasFilm had been one of the first to explore this idea with its "many-player online virtual environment" called Habitat. A few dozen people could play from home using Commodore 64 computers to interact with the others' online graphical representations, or avatars.

If Blaxxun's avatars were nothing compared with those of

Habitat, LucasFilm's world paled in comparison with the U.S. Defense Advanced Research Project's SIMNET, developed to conduct, among other things, war games. In one such game, more than two hundred military personnel around the world engaged in a virtual M-1 tank battle.

Although it was based in Munich, Blaxxun had staff in the San Francisco Bay Area to monitor developments in Silicon Valley. The company knew that these other organizations were far ahead of them. That meant nothing. What mattered was who came up with the best solution. The men of Blaxxun were supremely confident that they would.

The world of the avatar—even in its fledging state in this warehouse in Germany, was irresistible. Drawn in by the excitement of helping make a quantum step in computing, I soon left my job at PC Plus and joined the Blaxxun team.

The programming was very interesting, but even more so was the business philosophy behind the company. Whereas Bettina and I were committed to growing only as fast as our customer base, Blaxxun's strategy was to dip its bucket into the torrent of VC money, create a piece of breakaway technology, buy an insanely expensive marketing campaign, then sit back and watch the profits roll in. It seemed like a perfectly brilliant strategy.

Blaxxun served as a great example to Bettina and me of what running a business could be like: the excitement, the teamwork, the dedication to a technology that might be beyond the current understanding of the market.

We also learned that the technology behind the product is what holds the real value. When venture capitalists decided to invest in Blaxxun, they didn't base their decision on things like the number of customers, the size of the sales force, or whether the company was making money. They were investing in an idea. For us, Blaxxun offered a lesson in the value of intellectual property rights, even at the company then known as Visualizing Ideas Michael Jetter.

The prevailing business model for German technology companies at the time was not so much to constantly create new products. It was to create one, usually very large, complex product, then sell the services required to implement that software. Bettina and I knew we didn't want to follow that model. The Blaxxun model of constant innovation and pushing the limits of technology was much more alluring.

Watching Blaxxun's meteoric rise, we couldn't help but feel hopelessly old-fashioned: like the people who labored to dig the Panama Canal might have felt if they had climbed over the next ridge and discovered an army of bulldozers moving in a day the amount of dirt it had taken them years to remove.

While we spent our spare time sequestered in our tiny office gaining customers one at a time, Blaxxun was racing into the future with passion and excitement, working day and night in a warehouse resplendent with the latest computer equipment, blissfully unconcerned with such mundane things as customers or profits. Our hand-to-mouth existence seemed ludicrous.

But our technology was not simply an interesting idea we wanted to bring to market. It was something that was born in our hearts. MindManager's roots lay in my struggle for survival. Since then, we had sacrificed to nurture it to life. Now it had grown into something that people said was changing their lives, unlocking their creativity, getting them organized, making work actually fun. After all this, MindManager had become much more than just a piece of software. It had become a piece of us. ●

BY THE SPRING OF 1996, Bettina and I had finished our first MindMan update, version 2.0. For the first time, we added features that had been requested by customers. Version 1.0 was in black and white: customers wanted color. And for the first time we added priority icons (Priority #1, #2, and so on) so that users could create an order in which to accomplish tasks.

Just after we released 2.0, I got a phone call from Eric Greenberg at Netscape, who had a great idea I wished I'd thought of before we finished this version. Greenberg was conducting development work to help the average person gain access to the nascent Internet. Eric had learned about our software, liked it, and asked if we might be able to come up with a way to export MindMan content as Web pages. Netscape, based in Silicon Valley, was interested in creating a robust online world. A key component of that would be people's ability to easily post information to the Internet. Eric understood that the structure of the maps could provide an efficient way to model Web sites—as long as there was a way to turn the map content into HTML, the programming language used to create such sites.

Prior to Eric's call, an HTML export had never occurred to me: the Worldwide Web was, after all, still relatively new. But as soon as he raised the possibility of seeing maps as Web sites, I became obsessed with figuring out a way to do it.

In some ways we'd already started the process, having finished our first MindMan update—version 2.0. The map interface in this version was a simple hierarchy. The title at the center of the map was at the top of the information pyramid. Next came the branches, then the sub-branches, and so on. In the context of the Web, I figured that if the map title corresponded to the home page, each main branch corresponded to a section within the site and the sub-branches to pages within each section. Essential to the conversion from map to

Web site were text notes, blocks of text that could be attached to a branch. The text notes could contain the content of each page of the site. Now all I had to do was work out the code.

After working nights and weekends for four weeks, I had just about figured out how to convert the maps to HTML. I sent Eric a beta version, he made a few suggestions, and in another week I had our first map-to-HTML conversion. We integrated this feature into our software, and MindMan 2.1 was ready for the Web.

Eric liked the final product and that I had created it so quickly. He sounded me out on my interest in coming to the United States and working with Netscape. Silicon Valley was leading the charge to develop the Internet into the next mass communications environment, he argued, and Netscape was leading the movement. At the time, Netscape was working on the 3.0 version of its Internet browser, intent on giving Microsoft competition for ruling the desktop.

The idea of moving to the United States instantly appealed to both Bettina and me. In the first place, everyone agreed that America, and the Bay Area in particular, was the place to be in the mid-1990s if you were interested in computer technology. There lay all the excitement, all the new ideas—and all the money. Programmers from around the world were heading to California to stake their claim to untold riches.

But there were other, more personal reasons for us to consider leaving. Everyone we knew was busy living the German dream: working in one secure, traditional company or another, buying their first house, having their first children. We could never, would never belong to this world—and we found ourselves aspiring to it less and less. We had an opportunity now to take a leap into something entirely new.

I told the people at Blaxxun about my interest in joining the Internet gold rush. Franz Buchenberger, the CEO and president, pulled me aside and said, "You know, Mike, you don't have to leave the company just to go to America. You can keep working for Blaxxun, but at our office in San Francisco."

Franz arranged for me to spend the first week of May visiting

MIKE

the American office and seeing if it was really a place where Bettina and I could live. Two weeks later, I was on a plane headed for the Golden Gate.

The first time we had visited, everything about the Bay Area— the architecture, the ferries, the cable cars, the food, the palm-lined streets filled people from dozens of different cultures, made us want to return someday. Eight years later, with the city poised on the brink of the high-tech explosion, I couldn't imagine Bettina and me *not* living there. A few days later I flew home again and handed Bettina a gift-wrapped box. She unwrapped it, gave me a big hug, and put on her "I Love San Francisco" T-shirt.

Moving to California seemed a not terribly complicated project. We needed to lease our condo, pack up our things, get a couple of visas, and book a flight. How difficult could that be?

Within weeks, we found a Canadian couple who needed housing for two years while they worked at the International School in Starnberg. That took care of the condo. We had applied for H1B visas, a special category of visa that allows the holder to stay in the United States as long as six years, provided they are employed. We assumed we would have no problem whatsoever meeting the criteria. This turned out not to be true. I would have no problem: I was a highly trained, credentialed professional with a job waiting for me. Bettina's situation was more problematic. The business and marketing degrees she had earned in Germany had no clear equivalent in the American educational system. As such, it was harder for U.S. immigration officials to understand that she was, indeed, a fully trained professional.

Even thought Bettina had supported me for years while I finished my post-graduate work—not to mention the three years I was receiving and recovering from treatment—she was the one U.S. officials considered more of a risk. Without the precise equivalent of an American bachelor's degree, Bettina would have to prove to U.S. immigration officials she did in fact have a "career path," composed of relevant educational training and subsequent work experience.

Four times as thick as mine, Bettina's immigration application was complete with records going back to grade school, a complete work history since graduation from high school, and detailed letters of recommendation. It took her weeks to assemble the file. Once she submitted it, immigration officials told us it would take many more weeks to verify each document.

They told us the process would be even more prolonged because of the job Blaxxun had offered Bettina. Knowing she had gainful employment waiting for her was great for us in terms of having two incomes. But it meant that Blaxxun had to prove to U.S. officials that it had hired her because it could not find an American qualified to do the job.

With the Canadian couple due to arrive shortly, we realized we would never be able to go directly from Munich to San Francisco. So we did what any self-respecting, young Bavarian couple does under similar circumstances. We moved in with my parents.

One minute, Bettina and I had fancied ourselves as the thoroughly modern couple, jetting off to a new life amid the coffee shops and art galleries of San Francisco. Suddenly we were regressing to our childhoods. Rather than eating panini in North Beach, we were helping my mother make cookies. Instead of late nights at The Paradise Lounge, we were going to afternoon movies with Mom and Dad. Instead of wandering through the exotic flower conservatory at Golden Gate Park, I was mowing the lawn.

But it did give us time to work on our business. We were ready to start on version 3.0. This was another milestone for us. To our way of thinking, version 1.0 was proof that we could create mapping software. Versions 2.0 and 2.1 represented small refinements to the original product. But 3.0 would be our first fully conscious attempt to make a really great piece of software that met the real needs of real customers—that would enable users to edit maps much more quickly, customize them to a greater degree, and allow teams working in different locations to simultaneously edit the same map.

My mother and father were probably just as appalled as we were at having their son and daughter-in-law move in. But they were gracious hosts. The four of us managed to peacefully co-exist for a more than a month before we all began to go a little crazy. At that point, it became pretty clear that, no matter how much my parents loved us, Bettina and I were overextending our stay. So in early September, Bettina quit her job in the marketing department of a database company, I told Blaxxun that I would rejoin its team when and only when we made it to San Francisco, and, to my parents' great, if unspoken, relief, Bettina and I made plans to head back to our favorite part of Italy, Lago di Garda, for an undetermined stay.

Pineta Campi featured twenty tennis courts and proximity to Limone, the same town we had visited last time before chest pains sent us rushing back to Munich. It rented apartments by the week.

We borrowed my dad's new Audi sedan, loaded it with an ancient PC nicknamed Charlie Brown (because of the work I was doing at the time on pieces of computer code called "peanuts") and a few boxes of office supplies, and headed to Italy. We moved into camp, set up an office on the kitchen table, and got to work on MindMan 3.0. All that our little headquarters lacked was a way to contact resellers and customers.

To access our CompuServe account, we had to make a deal with the tennis camp management. For a few thousand lire a week, we were allowed to jack into the hotel reception desk phone line every second day and download our email. We would then answer the mail offline back at the kitchen table, return to the reception desk two days later, and send off our replies. So much for working at Internet speed.

This lack of a connection to the outer world bothered us only so much. The weather was wonderful this time of year; bright and sunny, with just a trace of autumn in the air. We managed to get in a game every now and then, though we both still preferred squash.

Most afternoons, when our energy flagged after a tough day at the office, we would stroll down the narrow streets between whitewashed walls and ornate iron fountains looking for fruits and vegetables for our evening meal. Except for the occasional veal parmigiana or meat-stuffed ravioli, we were still following a vegetarian diet. This quiet Italian atmosphere differed from our normal hectic pace, and we loved it.

The isolation of the Italian lake region gave us a chance to focus on version 3.0, to craft a development plan that would enable our

MindMan program to run circles around VisiMap, our only known competitor at this point. Here we imagined direct editing of map branches, new text note features, and a conference server to allow online collaboration.

We made great strides, but after about five weeks we realized that we had better get back to the real world. In the first place, our little respite was costing us a fortune. Then there was the unfinished matter of the visas. The United States issued ninety thousand H1B visas annually. Even so, there were far more people around the world who wanted to work in the United States.

We soon learned that we hadn't been among the lucky thousands and would have to reapply. At first, we thought that meant that Bettina would have to go through the application procedure all over again. Luckily, we could just resubmit the whole package. But it would take at least another month for the immigration office to process her new claim. Caught between here and there, we moved back in with my parents.

As a further enticement to me to stay with the company, Blaxxun hired Bettina to work in the company's Munich office, simplifying her visa application process. Then Blaxxun went a step further and hired a special attorney to accelerate the bureaucratic wrangling. One morning in early November, Bettina and I came to work to find our shiny new visas sitting on our desks.

And so it was that on November 14, 1996, I boarded a jet to San Francisco with Bettina and Charlie Brown, my creaky, hundred-megahertz relic of a PC that had been with me for so long that I couldn't leave it behind. The only way I could fit it into my carry-on bag was to remove the outer covering and expose the internal chassis. I wasn't sure if security would let me on the plane with such a suspicious piece of equipment, so I asked my father to wait outside in his car with one of our monitors. I was all set to have Dad carry in the monitor so that I could prove Charlie Brown was a computer. But after running the chassis through the X-ray machine, the guards waved us through.

Once in San Francisco, we took a cab to the apartment Blaxxun had reserved for us in the city's Fillmore neighborhood. We were surprised to find that not only was the apartment quite large and comfortably furnished, but the complex had a hot tub in the center of the outdoor common area. At that time, the only hot tubs we had ever seen were at health spas. What a concept, we marveled, to walk out of your home dressed in a bathing suit and robe and relax in a giant bathtub under the stars. Only in California.

That first night in San Francisco, we decided to go out for dinner and, by chance, chose a Mediterranean restaurant. For us Germans, Mediterranean basically meant Italian, so we expected pasta and zabaglione. But this restaurant featured real Mediterranean cuisine—grape leaves and hummus and babaganoush—and real belly dancers, which were about as common in Germany as hot tubs.

While the apartment was perfectly well furnished for business professionals who get up each morning and go off to work, it was less prepared for people with nighttime identities as software entrepreneurs. But by this time, having set up an office once in the isolation wing of a leukemia ward, in our Munich condo, at an Italian tennis camp, and twice in my parent's home, we were becoming quite good at it. Shortly after reporting for work at Blaxxun SF, we had our MindMan office up and running, thanks to folding tables and chairs from Office Depot.

With our duties at Blaxxun not too demanding, Bettina and I were able to spend a great deal of time on MindMan. We started to change the interface from our own unique design to a more officelike environment. Microsoft was becoming the de facto standard for desktop software. If we ever wanted MindMan to become mainstream software, we had to start making our interface look more like Microsoft's.

Life in San Francisco was a thrill. Each morning we took a brisk, scenic walk from the Fillmore to California Street and rode the cable car to work. Each night, we could choose from among hundreds of restaurants and bars, packed with sophisticated, stylish, go-getters having loads of fun. Before long, we felt like one of the crowd, residents of the best city on earth and ready to toast the New Year in America.

The Christmas holiday arrived and we took the occasional evening off from MindMan to stroll among the ornate stores surrounding Union Square, past the bustling restaurants of Chinatown and North Beach, and through Nob Hill's Huntington Park. The dozens of trees there were draped with thousands of tiny white lights and cast their soft glow on the spires of Grace Cathedral, towering across the street. This simple but powerful Gothic structure reminded us of home.

When the fire alarm went off in our apartment building at 6 o'clock Christmas morning, all we knew was that it sounded like something very bad was about to happen. Bettina jumped out of bed and started grabbing handfuls of important papers—visas, passports, MindMan financial records. I unplugged Charlie Brown, the laptop, the monitors, and the printer. Still in our pajamas, we raced out the door laden with our belongings—only to find our neighbors standing in their bathrobes with their arms draped over the railing, casually smoking cigarettes and chatting. They turned and looked at us like we were crazy, then went back to their conversations.

Before long we moved out of the city and into a waterfront apartment in the Marin County town of Tiburon, commuting each day by ferry. The daily trips back and forth across San Francisco Bay provided us with a complete and ever changing adventure. Each day we would sail past Alcatraz Island and the Golden Gate Bridge, past the banks of fog moving in off the ocean and over the hills of Marin County, past the giant flocks of cormorants and surf scooters. It was hard to believe we were doing something as banal as commuting when we were watching pelicans corkscrewing beak-first into the icy water, seals bobbing just yards from our speeding craft and—occasionally—gray whales spouting in the Pacific waters.

For forty-five minutes each morning, a fresh cup of ferry coffee warming our hands, we would brace ourselves against the frigid air and gaze dreamily at our new home. At the end of the day, with the city skyline illuminated, the shore necklaced by the lights of a dozen cities and the stars twinkling overhead, we almost had to pinch ourselves to realize that this was real. After so much stress and struggle, our new life suddenly seemed nothing short of magical. ◼

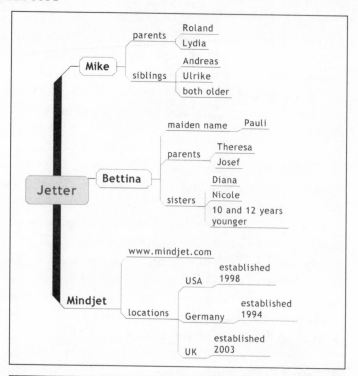

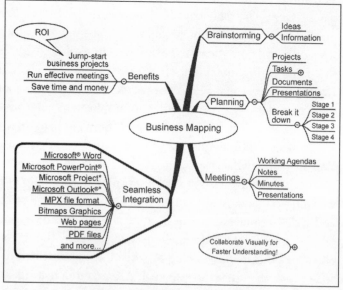

[TOP] Jetter map: an overview of our family

[BOTTOM] Business map: example of a MindManager X5 PRO map

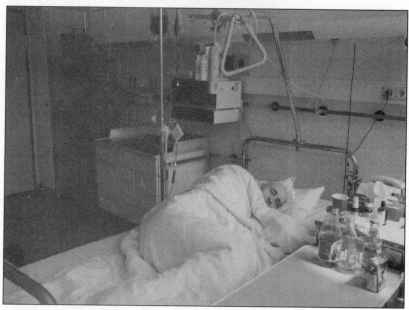

[TOP] We are getting married — June 4, 1988.
[BOTTOM] Mike in his hospital room at L21.

[TOP] Mike's family, from left to right: Mike, Bettina with niece Lucia, Lydia, Andi, Ruth, Viola, Roland, Uli, and Frederik.

[RIGHT] Bettina's parents, the Paulis

[TOP] The first office in our home in Tiburon.

[LEFT] We have visas!

Our office in Sausalito.

[TOP] The first convening of Mindjet's international force. From left to right: (standing) Lawrence Webb, Nick Duffill, Stein Asmul, Mike Jetter, Michael and Antje Louis (lower row) Bettina Jetter, Sigi Siegrist, Jeanne Daniele and Juergen Herzog

[BOTTOM] Bettina with Hobart Swan and her parents.

Celebrating at the "Entrepreneur of the Year" Awards from Ernst & Young.

the triathlon

21

Uli's Challenge

FOUR MONTHS AFTER we signed the lease on our Tiburon apartment, the same venture capitalists who gave Blaxxun the means to grow so quickly now wanted to focus exclusively on Europe. Bettina and I saw it coming, but it was still a shock to realize that by the summer of 1997, Blaxxun was going to retreat to Germany. If we chose to stay in the United States, we would be out of a job.

Lacking gainful employment, Blaxxun attorneys told us, our H1B visa would no longer be valid. In principle this meant we would have to leave the country immediately after the office closed, but they told us that we'd actually have ten days to wrap up our personal affairs. In nine months we had rented our condo, sold our car, moved in with my parents—twice—decamped to Lago di Garda, filed reams of visa paperwork, flown six thousand miles, lived in the Fillmore, bought a new car, moved to Tiburon, and bought a bunch of really ugly furniture. Now we might have to move again?

The attorneys told us we had one alternative. We could apply to have our H1B visa changed to a B2 tourist visa, which would allow us to stay in the States for another six months. The nice thing about this approach was that once we applied for the visa change, we could stay in the country until we got a response.

Two months later, we got our B2 visas. Thanks to a small stream of income from MindMan sales, we would be able to live in Tiburon and concentrate on our software business. As tourists, of course, we were not supposed to be conducting any business in the States: no marketing, no business cards, no flyers, no direct mail, no advertising. It was like being back in the tennis camp all over again, but with an ocean view and a hot tub.

For the next month and a half, Bettina and I toiled diligently, managing our ever growing circle of resellers and working toward version 3.0. My job was to focus on the core features of 3.0. Bettina was completing a German translation for a tool that would let our customers edit items in our Symbol Gallery.

Central to the mapping technique is the use of graphic elements to stimulate the right side of the brain. Thus far we had colored branches and text, as well as colorful priority icons. The symbols were another step in this direction, giving nonartists like me the ability to add memory-stimulating images such as stop signs, pocket watches, arrows, and even animals.

That first symbol gallery led us to a developer named Larry Daniele. We had created the symbols in a file format called metafile. The only tool I could find that would let users edit this kind of file was Larry's Metafile Companion. We soon put Larry on contract to help us create symbols for our gallery.

He was a good programmer and a great guy. Bearded and sprightly, he always had a droll comment to add to an otherwise dry technical discussion. Larry was soon guilty of a business apostasy that endeared us to him forever: he forgave us the last payment we owed him for work he had done. When we asked him why, he just said that he believed in the product. Letting us off the hook (at a time when we really needed a financial break like this) was his way of showing it.

Also on Bettina's list was the creation of our first online tutorials. Prior to the creation of MindMan, Bettina had never done any programming. Now here she was learning how to create online tutorials, animated viewlets that demonstrated visually to our Web site visitors exactly how to use the software.

One of our first real breaks for 3.0 came with a phone call from Peter Vieser, who worked for the Siemens, the German technology giant. Vieser was inviting me to present our software to a workshop being presented by Siemens, Intel, and Arthur Anderson Consulting. Vieser hoped to infect his American colleagues with the German enthusiasm for mind mapping, and wanted me to make the introduction using MindMan.

When Peter asked what it would cost for me to come and give the workshop on mapping, I hadn't the slightest idea what to charge. Plucking a number out of thin air, I said $5,000. After some back and forth, Peter and his employers agreed to my price—on the condition that I deliver to them within six weeks a working, pre-Alpha release version of our 3.0 software.

The workshop I gave was pretty bad. As I had never done such a thing before, I had no idea what I was doing, and I think I probably came off as unprofessional. First, I was underdressed: I presented this unexpected software to a slacks-and-business-shirts crowd dressed in my standard blue jeans, sneakers, and knit shirt. Although MindMan was used to create presentations, I inanely didn't think to use it. I thought I would have plenty to say, but once I got on stage my mind went blank. I stammered around for a half an hour before Peter came up and got me off the hook.

But I got excellent feedback on the software, which I was then able to incorporate into the final 3.0 release, and I established a strong relationship with Siemens. The next year, in fact, the German behemoth purchased seventy MindMan licenses. It has since purchased thousands more.

As much fun as we were having working on the software and developing business connections, Bettina and I knew our time in Tiburon couldn't last forever. Our B2 visas would soon expire and we'd have to return to Munich. Then Uli and her now three-year-old son, Frederik, visited. One beautiful September day during my sister's two-week stay, the three of us were sitting on our patio watching Frederik play with a little plastic dump truck. We told Uli that we planned to return to Germany. She looked at us like we were crazy. Pointing toward the bay she said, "The weather is fantastic. The Bay Area is incredibly gorgeous. Why leave?"

Bettina and I looked at each other as if dumbstruck. We had gone through so much work to get here, and had been here less than a year. Why leave? We'd have to return to Germany to reapply for another six-month tourist visa. But once we got it, we could come right back to our existing apartment and have another half-year to figure out what to do next.

On October 9, 1997, after much hard work, we released MindMan version 3.0. Our visas expired and our product complete, we paid a few months' rent in advance, parked our car in our garage, and hopped a plane to Munich.

22

Business Planning 101

OUTSIDE OUR GARRET WINDOW overlooking downtown Starnberg, winter had descended. The sky was a dull gray, the clouds pregnant with rain, the tree limbs shedding their leaves in the wind that whipped down the corridors of the city.

Our friend Reini Klein, Mike's good friend and erstwhile member of the Bone Marrow Olympics Training Team, and his wife, Catja, had offered us their uppermost floor of their three-story condo when we returned to Munich. As we worked one night in early November 1997, we could hear the muffled sounds of a lively discussion in progress among the people in the dining room below. Every now and then the voices would reach a crescendo and we could almost see the dinner guests wagging their bread sticks to underscore their points.

Only later did we learn that we were the reason for the ruckus. That night Reini was explaining to his dinner guests, this next generation of German business leaders, that while they were sitting around enjoying themselves, his buddy in the attic was at that very moment running an international high-tech business with employees and customers scattered all over the world.

Reini and Catja's attic wasn't fancy, just a mattress in the corner and a few tables. Each time we wanted to make phone calls or check email, we had to descend to the second floor and request permission to plug in. But it allowed us to keep up the semblance of a business.

For two months, Mike and I toiled away, reading customer feedback to our 3.0 release, finding programming bugs, building the next service pack (so customers could fix those bugs), and doing whatever marketing we could squeeze in until it was time to head back to San Francisco. Finally, our new tourist visas arrived and we could return "home." Two days later, in January 1998, we boarded a Lufthansa jet lugging a laptop that weighed as much as a cinderblock and had our new, powerful, professional MindMan 3.0 safely tucked away on the hard drive.

Back in our Tiburon apartment, we had three months either to figure out how to stay or to prepare to leave—this time for good. We soon found a good immigration attorney, made an appointment, and told him our story.

The attorney told us an E2 visa could be valid for up to five years. Once we got it, we would just have to prove that we ran an active business registered in the United States and capable of supporting more than one household. We would have to hire people here in the States, but not right away. Finally, we would have to give immigration authorities a five-year business plan.

First we had to establish the value of the business, which we would base on the intellectual property rights to the software. After talking with our resellers and some of our larger customers, we were able to come up with what we thought was a credible figure. These same resellers and customers also gave us letters of reference. We could hold off on hiring staff, so we focused next on creating a business plan.

As we contemplated what such a plan might contain, it struck us as preposterous to call our business a business at all. We had no office (well, no real office) and no employees—nothing but a piece of software and a small circle of resellers. Nonetheless, the immigration officials would want to know how this business of ours would grow over the next half decade.

We found a book called *How to Create a Business Plan* and got to work. Mike and I figured that two years from then we'd have another version of MindMan. We would probably increase our prices in a year or so. We had toyed with the idea of someday offering some sort of support maintenance contracts like other software companies did—so we added that to the plan. Then we tried to estimate how many people we would add to the payroll each year. Six weeks later, we had a plan that, at the time, we thought was wildly optimistic.

We were now ready to submit to the authorities a three-inch-thick visa application filled with our IP rights valuation; letters of reference; and a detailed, if speculative, five-year plan. We had just one more step to take: transfer the rights to our company from Germany to the United States. But to do this, we discovered, we needed to hire a special kind of attorney, one of which we found in Los Angeles. After reviewing our application, this second attorney promptly informed us that our chances of convincing immigration officials that we had a real business would be vastly improved if we could prove that we had a real office.

BETTINA

23 — Hawaii, Juarez, Paris? No problemo!

ONE FEBRUARY MORNING IN 1998, Mike and I started driving around a few Marin County towns just north of the Golden Gate Bridge, looking for office space. In downtown Sausalito, we saw a sign for space to lease above a café. We parked and climbed a set of outdoor wooden stairs, past a hot tub and outdoor dining area, and peered beyond the For Lease sign.

The office consisted of one big room with a small kitchen area, a fireplace, and a patio with bay view. The sign in the window instructed interested parties to call a particular real estate company during normal business hours.

As we started back down the stairs, we noticed a man dressed in coveralls walking out of a larger empty space and asked if we might see the inside of the small one. As I explained what we were looking for, he noticed our accent and said that his wife was German, too. We established an immediate rapport, he showed us the office, and we loved it. He agreed to tell the management that "a very nice couple" was interested in the space. Apparently his word was the only qualification we needed. A week later we had our office.

A few days after the lease closed, we took the ferry into the city and met with our immigration attorney. The first thing he told us was that he would need a $4,000 retainer to shepherd our E2 visa papers through the immigration service. Oh and by the way, he mentioned, we understood didn't we, that we would not be able to apply for the E2 from within the United States? We would have to make an appointment to have our application reviewed at a U.S. embassy in another country. He suggested Paris, where he said he had business acquaintances who could help us out. Fine, I said, do it.

In the meantime, we concentrated on setting up our new office. We purchased computers, phones, and fax machines; gathered all the office furniture we had accumulated in our short stay in the States;

printed up new business cards; and began to reach out for the first time as an American company to our U.S. customers.

It was now the end of March 1998. As it happened, we had long since booked tickets to Hawaii. We probably should have just skipped it and focused on getting out E2 visas, but we couldn't bear the thought of forfeiting both our plane fare and hotel reservations simply because we should be going east to Paris not west to Oahu.

So off we went to Hawaii. We spent the first few days organizing our imminent trip to Paris, working with our attorney and his associates to schedule an appointment at the U.S. consulate there, booking flights and a hotel. But it was no use, our attorney told us. It was impossible to get an appointment. Perhaps Mexico, he suggested. Fine. Mexico.

Back to the phones in our hotel room we went, talking with the attorney, booking flights, and finding accommodations south of the border. The stress was exactly what Mike didn't need, and I began to worry that it was taking a toll on him. All he wanted to do was sleep, and he started getting that gaunt look on his face I had seen too many times before. He needed to drink Mai Tais, lie in the sand, and wiggle his toes in the water again. But it wasn't going to happen. We were too busy with logistics to lie on the beach.

On April 5, after five days stuck in our hotel room overlooking Waikiki Beach, we boarded a plane from Honolulu to San Francisco, then a few days later another one from San Francisco to El Paso, Texas.

Soon we were crossing the Rio Grande in our rental car into Juarez where, if all went well, we would receive a visa from the American consulate. The plan our attorney had devised called for us to spend one night in a hotel, then wait out front the next morning until an unnamed man drove up in a station wagon. For $500 in cash this person was going to drive us across town to the embassy and guide us through the visa process.

What roused us from our sleep was not so much the din of the traffic two floors below our hotel room, but the overpowering smell of diesel fumes. We got up, dressed in light clothes, and walked downstairs for fruit, toast, and coffee on the patio. As we ate, we scanned the crowd for a man looking for someone.

About 10:30, we noticed a beat-up station wagon pulling up to our hotel. A man got out, leaned against his car, and surveyed the group of tourists sitting on the patio. He must have been able tell by the look on our faces that we were the ones he was supposed to meet. He walked up to us and solemnly asked us if we were the Jetters. When we nodded, he broke out into a huge toothy grin and shook our hands. In halting English, he waved us toward the car, pried open the rusty back door, and waved us in.

After a ten-minute drive through belching buses, meandering pedestrians, and the complete lack of anything resembling ordinary traffic rules, we arrived at an unmarked building. Our guide walked us inside, got some paperwork from the top of a counter, and instructed us to sign at the bottom.

Needless to say, the forms were in Spanish. We had no idea what they were. We signed the forms, which he gathered up and, gesturing for us to follow him, carried into another building.

The good news was that this second building had a sign in English: United States Consulate, Ciudad Juarez—the first indication that we probably were in the process of getting a visa. The bad news was that there was a line emerging out the front door of the consulate, down the street, and around into an alley.

Our guide turned to us and whispered "No problemo." He led us up to the front of the line, told us to wait right there, then went off to chat up the guards. A few minutes later, he came back, put us in a very short line, said he would see us again in six hours, and disappeared.

This short line moved quickly and, upon reaching the counter, we were relieved of our papers and sent to a second and then, finally, a third line. Within an hour of our arrival we sat facing a very nice American woman who, as luck would have it, had not only been born in Germany but had vacationed in Starnberg just two years before. We were long-lost friends.

After reviewing our forms, she told us indifferently that there were some minor problems with our application—nothing she couldn't fix in a jiffy. "Go have a nice long lunch," she smiled. "I'll take care of this."

We left the coolness of the consulate and plunged into the heat of high noon in Juarez, wandering the noisy, chaotic streets in search of a restaurant. We finally settled on a little place that, despite its being mid-April, was choked with Christmas decorations. Every square inch of window, wall, and ceiling was festooned with dusty plastic evergreen boughs, gleaming red and green Christmas balls, and strobing Christmas lights. We sat at a small bar for a half an hour, sipping weak Palomas and killing time. Then we sat down for chicken mole, rice, and guacamole washed down with *horchata*, a sweet, iced cinnamon-almond drink. We sat there trying to eat as slowly as we possibly could and managed to kill another hour before we gave up and rushed back to the consulate.

We checked back in with the woman, who smiled and told us to take a seat until our names were called. Fifteen minutes later we had two five-year E2 visas to the United States of America. What amazing news. We thought we would probably get the standard one-year visas or, at best, visas good for two years. The maximum of five years was a godsend.

A few minutes later, our driver returned, carrying two bottles of tequila. At first we thought he was going to help us get drunk and celebrate our new visas. But it turned out that the liquor was for his friends, the guards.

All we had to do now was make it back to the hotel, pack our bags, and drive back across the border. Leaving Mexico required only that we endure a half hour of sitting in line, engines running, going nowhere. Entering America, on the other hand, was not quite so simple. The U.S. Customs officer who leaned down from the booth and stuck his face into the car looked about eighteen years old. He surveyed our documents, and asked us where we came from and where we were going.

"How long do you plan to stay in the U.S.?" he asked Mike brusquely. Because we knew the visa allowed us to stay for five years, Mike acted very blasé and replied, "Oh, we don't know exactly. We'll have to see."

I was afraid that Mike was going to get us into trouble and tried to discreetly nudge him with my elbow. The officer gave Mike a long look, then stepped down from the booth and began walking around the car, peering into the windows. After he had returned to Mike's window, he took another look at our visas and then, as if at a complete loss, turned to another agent and said "What's an E2?" The other agent, older and obviously more experienced, said "Don't worry about them. Those E2 people are always going back and forth across the border. Just stamp the passport."

I reached over, reclaimed our new visas, and gestured to Mike to get going before he uttered more nonsense. ■

May Day

BETTINA AND I HAD PURCHASED nonrefundable tickets to Paris. We didn't need to go, but decided to anyway. It would give us a chance to check in with associates in Munich, for one thing.

In the more than four years since my first relapse, I had made a point of dropping by Station L21 to see Dr. Ledderose every time I was home. We would discuss my current state of health, and he would fill me in on the latest developments in leukemia treatment. I would also get a blood test while I was there—the results of which Dr. Kolb always liked to add to his research database. But the May 4 blood test showed that my white blood cell count was forty thousand per microliter. While we were running around trying to straighten out our immigration status, I had considered in passing that the stress might not be good for my health. I should have trusted my instincts: the stress had pushed me into relapse number two.

The night after we learned the results, Bettina and I went to see *Titanic*, which had just been released. As we left the theater, we weren't the only ones crying. But we weren't shedding tears for the late lamented hero. We had tried anything and everything in the last eight years. I had had two bone marrow transplants. I had become one of the first people to receive a donor leukocyte injection. And I had made myself a guinea pig for the stem-cell approach. If I was really having a second relapse, what treatments were left—if any?

I continued to reflect on the reality of the blood test: so far, I had lived eight mostly good years since my diagnosis. This is much longer than the average CML patient could have expected at the time, and I had enjoyed generally good health. After having gone more than four years without problems, I had been tempted to think my CML was in the past. But in the back of my mind, I kept reminding myself that I would not live out a normal life span. If the disease didn't get me, I figured, all the drugs, radiation, and chemotherapy I had been given surely would. In the best case scenario I gave myself twenty more years; in the worst case, ten. If the later were true, I had two more years. Did I dare hope to reach the grand old age of thirty-seven?

When we met with Dr. Ledderose the next day, he was clearly upset at this latest news, though he tried to lighten the mood. But we knew from a long time ago that any time he started pushing the hair back off his forehead, he was struggling to say something, thinking hard to find a way to put my latest remission in the best possible light.

He began by reminding me that the course of my illness had not been normal. The DLI and stem-cell treatments I gotten after my first relapse had given me better chances at survival than patients just a year earlier never had. At that time, they were still considered experimental. But these treatments were now widely used, he said.

I asked him what he had up his sleeve next. He looked down and laughed and began fooling with his hair again. After a moment he looked up and said that he and Dr. Kolb had discussed my relapse in considerable depth the night before. The body of knowledge surrounding these other treatments had grown significantly since they had tried them on me, he said. And there were new drugs on the market that looked very promising. But after looking at all the alternatives, he and Dr. Kolb were recommending that we start with another round of donor leukocyte injections, much like he and Kolb had given me last time.

Since the first time they gave me DLI in October 1993, the two doctors had done a great deal of research on DLI and were finding it increasingly successful in treating chronic myeloid leukemia relapses. It hadn't appeared to work for me five years earlier, but they were confident it would work now.

As with the last time, this would be just a straight injection of Andi's white blood cells, which would be filtered out of his blood. There would be no radiation therapy or chemotherapy. I would begin taking interferon alpha again to stimulate my immune system. But the dosage would be too low to cause side effects.

As Ledderose described the treatment, Bettina and I relaxed a bit. It would be a familiar and painless, if time-consuming procedure. In fact, it would consume about two months, Dr. Ledderose said. In the meantime, Bettina and I would have to continue paying rent on our California apartment and on our new Sausalito "office"—at that point just an empty room. And the clock would continue to tick on our new five-year E2 visas.

I entered the hospital as an outpatient on Monday, May 11, 1998. Back to Munich came Andi and his white blood cells. A few hours later, another liter and a half of Andi's blood was running through my veins.

Dr. Ledderose discharged me that night and told me that I could do what I pleased for about six weeks. By then, he said, Andi's white blood cells would have become established and would start attacking the leukemic cells. At this point I would need to stay close to Munich in case I had any health problems. If, as had happened during the first donor-leukocyte treatment, Andi's cells started attacking my marrow again, I would need to be close by.

In the interim, Ledderose said, I could return to the United States, but I needed to make sure I returned in July, before I became too vulnerable to infection. If I waited too long, then caught a cold on the flight back, it might be the last cold I ever caught. ▪

the new beginning

Mindjet

WHAT WEATHER JUNE WILL BRING to the San Francisco Bay Area depends on where you live within the region. Most of the city was foggy, the residents bundled up in heavy coats. Across the bay in Sausalito, life was a little better. Half of the town, the part closest to the Golden Gate Bridge, was in the same fog bank. Just a few blocks north, though, the afternoon sun was shining into the window of our new, six-hundred-square-foot office above the Caledonia Kitchen café. I looked out my window at leaves on the trees that circled City Hall and the adjacent park. A couple of kids were playing basketball. The bay waters just across Bridge Way from our window were tranquil, the rigging on the hundreds of sailboats moored beside the boathouse neighborhood banging gently against aluminum masts.

Mike and I had just finished turning the kitchen area into our computer-equipment room when the phone rang. It was Preben Gammelmark from Hewlett-Packard Germany. He said he was in San Francisco and wondered whether he might drop by the next day to talk about some possible business opportunities with his company. Nine tomorrow morning? Of course, I replied enthusiastically.

After I hung up, Mike and I just stood there and looked around at our threadbare little billet. How in the world were we ever going to pull off a visit from a representative of one of the largest technology companies on the planet, a company with which we were very anxious to do business?

First of all, we had neither the chairs nor the table large enough to accommodate three people: either we go out that night and find one somewhere, or one of us would have to spend the entire meeting leaning nonchalantly against a wall. Then there was the air conditioner that made the whole floor vibrate: we would have to hope for a cool day. Finally, there was the very ugly rash that had recently appeared on both of Mike's arms. It looked so inflamed, so angry, that we thought for a moment of calling back and canceling the meeting. But it's not like someone from HP would just drop in again next week.

Concerned that more stress would only make Mike's skin condition worse, I drove him home at about six that evening and headed for Office Depot. I found a table and four chairs, but because our car was so small, I had to make three trips from the store to get it all to our office. Then I had to screw the whole thing together.

Luckily, the next day dawned overcast and windy. Mike was able to wear a long-sleeve shirt and kept his hands below the table. The meeting with Preben went off without a hitch. It didn't result in any immediate sales, but it helped forge a relationship, however unequal, between our two companies. (Like Siemens, HP has since become one of our best customers.)

Able to get back to work again for the first time since before we had left for Hawaii, Mike and I jumped into action after our guest departed. We had a lot to do. We needed to start establishing a U.S. presence, and we had to keep moving forward on our version 3.5, which we planned to release that fall.

Our 3.5 version to-do list included more and better symbols and new features such as find-and-replace and spell checking that continued our push toward a more Office-like environment. We also introduced floating symbols.

By now, we were creating MindMan in German, English, and French. Each new feature had to be done almost in triplicate—as did all of the help files and tutorials. It was a lot of work for Mike and me to manage while jetting back and forth across the Atlantic for tests and treatments. But in our new office, and without other major distractions for a month, we were able to make considerable progress on MindMan 3.5.

Then, suddenly, it was July and time to return to Munich before Mike became too vulnerable to infection. We got in touch with a German acquaintance who agreed to help us out and make the office look like someone was actually using it while we were gone. We gave her the office key, locked up our Tiburon apartment, put the car back in the garage, took a cab to SFO and flew back to Munich, prepared to stay there for as long as it took Mike to regain his health.

As luck would have it, it had been almost exactly two years since we had leased our condominium to the Canadian couple. We needed a place to live and work in Munich while the treatment ran its course. So we reclaimed the condo.

With a burst of excitement on the flight to Munich, we christened our new company Mindjet ("mind" as in thinking and mind mapping; "jet" as in Jetter, but also as in to move quickly, to accelerate). But between Mike's relapse, our visa escapades, and the constant travel, no excitement could mask our fatigue. Exhaustion was dangerous to Mike's health. Running an international business was wearing us down. We needed a new plan to go along with the new name.

One of the hardest things we had faced since moving to the States was managing a business that broke down into two main markets: Europe, and everywhere else on the planet. We felt we could manage one market. Trying to handle them both was depleting us. We needed to shift responsibility for the European market to someone else. That would mean losing control and revenue, but we felt we had no other choice. If we were serious about making a real impact on the software market, we had to have an American presence. We couldn't do that from Germany. On the other hand, the revenue from our European sales kept us afloat. There was no way we could abandon that market. If our business was to flourish, we would have to make our most difficult decisions yet. We needed to share our precious little jewel.

We decided to start by assembling a list of all the German resellers and software companies with whom we had worked over the past few years. Then we winnowed that list down to four we felt would be best suited to manage and grow our European sales. In four separate meetings held all over Germany, we explained to these companies our plans for carving off the European market. When we finished our presentation, we asked each company, if interested, to make a formal presentation on how it would manage its part of the business.

A company called MarketSoft, based in Alzenau, just outside of Frankfurt, had been one of our most successful resellers. Among other attractions, it had set up its own fulfillment system to ship products directly to clients. When we met with them a week later, managing directors Michael Louis and Jürgen Herzog impressed us a great deal.

Michael clearly felt the most passionate about MindMan. About Mike's height, with a bushy head of brown hair, wireless rim glasses, and a smile that lit up his face, he was full of enthusiasm for the project. He loved to laugh and said he loved to dance, too. But this meeting revealed the more somber side of this married father of two young children. Michael had a good head for business—when it was time for business.

Jürgen was more reserved. He and Michael had built their company together, but he seemed tentative about exploring a relationship with our company. A large, stocky man with short gray hair, Jürgen and his wife loved all things Italian. They spoke it fluently, and had a fantasy about moving there someday with their young daughter. He didn't seem, though, to have much of a fantasy about working with us.

Yet we persisted, noting that, like us, MarketSoft was a small company, so the playing field was level. Michael in particular seemed to understand the goals we had in mind for our software. He had many innovative ideas on how to expand the market. In what we took as a good sign, we also learned that Michael had once worked for a company located in the county directly north of Marin.

The timing for this new relationship was good. It was now early July 1998. Our plan was to release the 3.5 version of our software in October. At that time, we would also announce that we were changing the product name from MindMan to MindManager. (A marketing partner of ours recommended that we drop the name MindMan, saying would never fly in the States. American customers coming across a product called MindMan would immediately wonder "Was this a product for men only? What about women?")

By choosing a European partner at this point, we could simultaneously announce the name change, officially unveil the new company called Mindjet, and introduce the exclusive MindManager reseller for German-speaking countries.

There was one wrinkle in our full-throttle plans: Mike's relapse and recent DLI treatment. Dr. Ledderose was confident that Mike's condition would stabilize as Andi's leukocytes gathered enough momentum to start destroying the aberrant cells. But there was always a chance that, as in his first relapse, Andi's leukocytes would either do nothing or too much: either prove unable to gain the upper hand on the leukemia or become so vigorous that they began attacking Mike's bone marrow.

In any case, Mike was entering the critical phase of the DLI. Andi's white blood cells, buttresses by the interferon, would, we hoped, begin waging war on Mike's immune system.

After much debate, Mike and I decided not to tell our new partners at MarketSoft that we would develop this latest version of MindManager while Mike was in the middle of a leukemia relapse. We felt confident enough in his prognosis to enter into a business relationship revealing a great deal about our company to Michael and Jürgen—but nothing about Mike's health.

Dr. Ledderose closely monitored Mike through the rest of July and into August to make sure his blood values stabilized. In late August, we signed the agreement with MarketSoft, with a planned October 9 release date for version 3.5. By early September, Mike's blood count looked good and we readied ourselves to fly back to the States.

But at the end of September, Mike's white blood cell count suddenly dropped below two thousand. Once again, the DLI hadn't worked. I was panic-stricken and afraid. Mike was furious, frustrated, and depressed. ●

Office of the 21st Century

BETTINA AND I HAD ENTERED Dr. Ledderose's office expecting him to give me a clean bill of health so that we could go back to San Francisco and start building our business. We left knowing that I would have to return to the hospital for my third bone marrow transplant. No, there wouldn't be radiation or chemo. Yes, I could take my computer with me and finish up version 3.5 without interruption.

But I would be stuck here in Munich for another two months just as the weather here was getting dreary—and just as the golden light of Northern California's Indian Summer was coming into full glory. At this time of year, the weather in the Bay Area is incomparable. The days are still warm, but there is a hint of autumn in the evening air. The fog that persecuted San Franciscans all summer long lifts. At dusk, the grass that blankets the hills around the bay takes on an orangeish hue, contrasting sharply with darkening blue of the sky. Autumn had become my favorite time of year in California, and I didn't want to miss it—and not just because I like to look at pretty sunsets.

Since this struggle against CML began, I had become much more sensitive to the weather. With my immune system in a constant state of compromise, I was much more susceptible to colds and flus. Any time I had to spend late fall, winter, or spring in Germany, my risk of getting ill increased. I wanted to get back to California not only because I loved it and wanted to get back to work, but because I wanted to avoid the restaurants, elevators, and movie theaters full of my sniffling, sneezing fellow countrymen.

Having to undergo a third bone marrow transplant also meant that Andi would have to come down from Zurich for the sixth time. For the third time, Dr. Ledderose would have to put Andi under general anesthesia and puncture his pelvic bones to extract the marrow. This was a lot to ask—even of your own brother.

I hid my rage from Dr. Ledderose because I knew he was doing the best he could. The course of my disease hadn't been normal. I'm sure it must have been frustrating for him to have a patient who always appeared to respond to well to treatment, only to suffer relapse after relapse. All the same, I couldn't believe that the DLI had failed. It had been almost five years since they gave me my first donor-leukocyte injection. Hadn't they learned anything in those five years?

I tried not to dwell on the disappointment and to just prepare to go in again. One benefit of having spent so much time in the leukemia ward was that I was able to get a few extra things to help make the time pass more quickly. After my second relapse I had been able to snag a table and chair. This time, if I was going to finish version 3.5 on time, I would need more. I needed an ISDN line that would give me high-speed access to the Internet. When I made this request to Dr. Kolb, he just shook his head in disbelief and said he would arrange it.

Once equipped, I could stay in constant contact with the developers who were working on the version 3.5 from workstations around the world. When we finished the newest version, I would be able to post it to our Web site, get it to all our resellers to package for their customers, and answer customers' questions about the new release— all from the hermetic confines of my isolation room. Bettina, meanwhile, worked from our condo on marketing and public relations—from packing the new version, to preparing tutorials and screen shots to presenting MindManager 3.5 to the media.

In the end, the launch went off without a hitch. No one, not even MarketSoft, had any idea what had gone on behind the scenes. To our partners, our resellers and our customers, this had been just another normal product release.

In the immediate aftermath of my bone marrow transplant, Dr. Kolb, Dr. Ledderose and the team of physicians couldn't agree on whether I needed to be in the isolation room, or whether I could simply get the transfusion and go home. From the first day I was admitted, my count of two thousand white blood cells per microliter was

MIKE

higher than it was when they discharged me after my first transplant. True, they had never given anyone a bone-marrow transfusion on an outpatient basis, but then no one had ever been transfused as many times as I had. With no clear precedent, the argument went back and forth—until one of the doctors pointed out that any problems with my "premature" discharge might have negative implications for the hospital's medical insurance rates. That settled it. Even though I seemed otherwise perfectly healthy, I would stay in isolation until further notice.

After two weeks, though, Dr. Ledderose came in and told me that it just didn't make sense for me to stay any longer. He reminded me that I still needed to obey the rules regarding exposure to children, pets, potted plants, and even the most minor diseases. I needed to continue to take my medications, he said, and to avoid sunlight and stress.

One of the medications I was taking was interferon alpha, the same drug I had taken periodically since my first diagnosis, an overdose of which had led to the chest pains that sent Bettina and me driving madly back from Italy eight years before. I had since learned a great deal about proper dosages of this drug. Interferon alpha never cured me, but it was very useful at those times when I needed to make my immune system just a little bit stronger, when I needed to survive beyond the hospital walls.

In mid-December 1998, after three months of shuttling between the leukemia ward and our old condo, Bettina and I packed up our office supplies and computers and prepared to head back to San Francisco.

The day before we left, though, we learned that our software had just won an award from the prestigious Fraunhofer Institute. The institute sought out technology that would comprise part of the "Office of the 21st Century." This great honor was a boon to our European sales. The only catch was that the award ceremony was a little more than a month away and would take place here in Germany.

There was no way we could miss an award presentation like this. After being back in the States barely a month, we got back on a plane, flew into Frankfurt early one morning, immediately caught a train to Stuttgart, arrived at our hotel in the afternoon, took a two-hour nap, got up, got dressed, went to the ceremony, collected our award, and went out to celebrate with Michael, Jürgen, and my parents. We got back to our hotel very late, awoke at 6:00 a.m., caught the train back to Frankfurt, jumped back on the plane, and flew home. The entire trip, including two twelve-hour flights, took just forty-eight hours. We should have gotten an award for that, too!

(27) Building a Family

THE TRIP, IF SLIGHTLY HARROWING for a man in Mike's delicate condition, was well worth it. The award seemed to act as a catalyst. Working with a marketing consultant in the States, Mike and I were able to generate much greater media interest, which in turn brought new customers flooding in from America and around the world.

To handle this new work load, we made another great leap forward in the summer of 1999—hiring our first employees. We did so with some trepidation. Having employees would bring a whole host of new problems: paperwork, liability issues, tax headaches. There would be benefits to provide, processes to establish, and rules to enforce. There would be time spent training people. And there would be employee turnover. But there was no way we could do all that needed to be done to storm the U.S. beachhead. We needed help, and lots of it.

Our first office employee was Giovanna Helena Vitau, whom we brought on board in November to manage the office. A lovely woman in her late forties, Giovanna reminded us both in appearance and sensibilities of the French actress Jeanne Moreau. Short, with blond hair, blue eyes, and full lips, Giovanna was a product of the 1960s in America, a true San Francisco flower child. She was free-spirited, loved life, and devoured champagne. At the same time, she was what they call in baseball a "utility player." She could do accounting, type incredibly fast, make travel arrangements, and keep the office organized. But more than any of that, Giovanna embodied the sense of politeness, openness, and tolerance that we wanted our entire company to project.

Larry Daniele, whom we had first hired as a consultant to help us improve the symbol gallery, soon went from contractor to full-time staff. He continued to work from his Boston home, as did his wife, Jeanne, whom we then hired to create online instructional materials.

Jeanne, a slim brunette with fine features and demure smile, was even more gregarious than her wise-cracking husband.

Londoner Nick Duffill signed on to provide technical support to Larry and Mike. Nick was a skilled and inventive software consultant, a pleasant person to work with, and, as Mike and I marveled, "scary smart."

Stein Azmul worked with us from his native Norway to help Mike research ideas for future product features. When we met him, we were surprised at how young Stein was. With classic Nordic features and a long brown ponytail, Stein typified the kind of techie who melded work with life; creating, for example, a large and complex mind map of *Star Trek* minutiae.

That summer it occurred to Mike and me that while hiring employees met one of the key tests essential to keeping our E2 visas legal, none of these employees had ever met. So we invited everyone on an all-expenses-paid trip to California. While none of them knew anything of the personal challenges we had faced over the last decade, Mike and I wanted them to come together and help us celebrate the improbable creation of this thing called Mindjet.

Everyone began arriving in San Francisco on October 12, 1999. Larry and Jeanne flew in from Boston. Michael Louis; his wife, Antje; and Jürgen Herzog came from Germany. Stein flew in from Norway and Nick Duffill from London. Two of our resellers, Sigi Siegrist from RES-Software in Switzerland and Lawrence Webb from M-Urge in London, rounded out the group.

This international team spent a week in the Bay Area. The visit started with a few days of business meetings at our Sausalito office, which was now the official, non-hospital room, non-condo, non-tennis camp, non-apartment, non-attic, non-childhood-bedroom Mindjet office.

Toward the end of the week, Mike and I rented a white stretch limousine. We then shepherded the entire group up north to Napa and Sonoma counties for a day of vineyard touring, wine tasting, and fine dining. By the time the visit ended, we had a unified team with a shared vision of Mindjet's future.

Business continued apace into 2000. In Europe, we now had installed MindManager licenses in Fortune 500 companies like SAP, Siemens, Hewlett-Packard, DaimlerChrylser, Unilever, and Oracle. The software, once conceived as a tool to help individuals work more creatively and productively, had blossomed into a full-fledged tool for large corporate teams. MindManager still helped people build visual mind maps of information and ideas—but we now referred to them as "business maps" because of how far they had evolved from the simple pen-and-paper maps Tony Buzan had created thirty years earlier. Instead of one person building a map to capture his or her own thoughts, a group of people could sit in a conference room and use a projector to view a map on a large screen. As the team brainstormed about a new project or product, or as they tried to improve an existing process, one person would use a keyboard to capture all those ideas in a map.

We got great feedback from this team process. First, MindManager created a transparent meeting in which everyone could see what was being discussed, decided, and assigned. It kept all participants on the same page (or screen). MindManager also served as a concise way to document the meeting. Five minutes after leaving the conference room, meeting participants would have a copy of the meeting notes sitting in their email inboxes—as a business map, a Microsoft Word document, a PowerPoint presentation, or a Web site. It was boosting productivity in many ways. And people still found it fun to use.

At the same time that we were becoming increasingly popular among large European customers, we also began to see the first fruits of our effort to get the attention of so-called early adopters in the United States, those brave souls committed to finding and using new technologies. In our case, these pioneers had ranged from independent business consultants like Tony Dottino of Dottino Consulting in New York and Cliff Shaffran of Quicksilver in Hong Kong to corporate clients like Sempra Energy, Hewlett Packard, DFS Group Ltd., and Consolidated Edison of New York.

These pioneers had bought early versions of the software and had helped us expand MindManager use within their respective organizations. They also created real business applications for our software. Tony and Cliff were busy showing large organizations how to use the mapping technique to conduct more efficient planning and to run better meetings. Jim Winninger found great interest within Sempra for a tool that quickly and easily created presentations and teaching modules. Debby McIsaac told us that, among other uses, MindManager had enabled her to double the meeting participation among her international group of Hewlett Packard consultants. Ron Glickman and Rick Hamilton ushered in a new era of efficiency and collaboration within the IT division of the luxury retail giant DFS, which has since expanded MindManager use across the organization.

Al Homyk and David Hill, working with Dottino Consulting, used MindManager to implement a zero-based budgeting program that has saved Con Edison millions each year in improved business processes. Equally important, they said, was the way MindManager was causing a cultural shift within the thirteen-thousand-person utility company. The map interface helped even the Luddites understand how their job fit into a larger whole. Gaining this understanding made Con Edison employees more willing than ever before to work together to identify and solve business problems.

Of all the things we had heard from our customers, this last was perhaps the most exciting. Coming so many years after I first carried Mike's computer into Station L21, Con Edison's experience was real-life vindication of our mission to create a new way for people to work together in more creative, efficient ways.

The practical uses for MindManager created by this visionary cast of early adopters would be critical to Mindjet's ability to move to the next stage of growth. But we had to move beyond these customers. These people could clearly see the advantages of using MindManager. But they were few in number. Our much larger market would be a second group: the "pragmatists"—those who would adopt new technology only after someone else had shown them how they would benefit by doing so. Whatever these kinds of clients lacked in vision, the pragmatists were important to us because they were much more numerous. If we could figure out how to convince these slower-to-adopt clients that they would benefit from the software, then we could get MindManager out to many more hundreds of thousands of users—perhaps, someday, to millions.

Then, in May 2000, we hit a speed bump. Michael Louis and Jürgen Herzog had come to the conclusion that they could best serve their customers by creating their own new software product. The product would be based on MindManager, they said, but better suited to meet the particular needs of their European clients.

This strategy posed an obvious problem. How could we support a change in direction in which MarketSoft would use the revenues it got from selling MindManager to create a competitor? Yet MarketSoft had done a tremendous job of pushing our software into the European market. Michael and Jürgen had indeed understood their market and how to increase our presence in it, but now they wanted to increase their presence instead.

Four months later, Michael, Jürgen, Mike, and I gathered together at the MarketSoft office Alzenau for a birthday party. There was a chocolate sheet cake with buttercream icing, decorated with two logos. Though the final papers would not be signed and sealed until eight months later, that cake celebrated not so much a birthday as a birth: in spirit, if not yet by the letter of the law, Mindjet and MarketSoft were now one. After much debate and negotiation, Mike and I had merged our Mindjet with Michael and Jürgen's MarketSoft to form a new and stronger Mindjet with seventy employees and offices on two continents. ●

MINDJET HAS CONTINUED TO THRIVE. In 2001, we finally decided to raise venture capital funding so we could expand more aggressively into the American market. In 2002, we delivered our first Pocket PC and Palm OS versions. In April 2003, we launched our first Tablet PC application. Because it has been received by the media and industry analysts as one of the best applications for this new computing platform, MindManager for Tablet PC has gained us greater visibility among business users. At the same time, it has let us forge stronger alliances with Microsoft and many of the key computer makers. These organizations are heavily invested in the success of the Tablet PC, and see our software as one of the most compelling reasons for customers to replace aging laptop PCs with Tablet PCs. Once again we are in the territory of those early adopters. If these more adventurous business professionals find Tablet PCs interesting enough to champion their adoption, MindManager will gain greater market share and visibility among the major players in the computing industry.

In September 2003, we reached a new milestone with the release of MindManager X5, an entirely new generation of the software that makes it easier for users to bring other forms of information and data in and out of the map interface. X5 represents Mindjet's first successful attempt to make the maps "smart." Previous to X5, the only way for users to get information into a map was to enter it themselves. Thanks to X5's XML-based design, users can now design map branches to reach into a wide variety of databases. These intelligent map parts can automatically populate a map with everything from financial data to the results of Web searches to RSS news feeds.

Representing an investment of millions of dollars, X5 is the first fully rearchitected version of MindManager since 1994, when Mike wrote the original MindMan code in his isolation room at L21. A truly international team of Mindjet developers worked for more than two years to remake MindManager, creating in the process a more elegant graphic user interface, support for Unicode, and a revamped Web site export. MindManager X5 and X5 Pro will help Mindjet get ever closer to its goal of gaining major desktop market share.

As a company, Mindjet continues to grow as well. Now there are nearly one hundred of us working in offices on three continents. Michael Louis, who first impressed us so much when we searched for someone with whom to share our fledgling business, has since joined Mike and me as a Mindjet co-director. Jürgen Herzog left in 2002, but Michael's business acumen and creativity have helped us penetrate the European market. Under his leadership, MindjetEU, the division of our company based in Alzenau, Germany, has grown each year. He has also led our initiative to open a new Mindjet office in London, which will serve our British and Scandinavian customers. More important to us and the way we try to conduct our business, Michael has become a close friend and trusted partner.

I always tried not to dwell on it, but before we merged with MarketSoft, there was always in the back of my mind the possibility that I might someday have to run Mindjet all by myself. I sleep more easily now knowing that if the worst should happen, I have help. ■

BETTINA

Epilogue: Mike

IT HAS BEEN FIVE YEARS since my last relapse and Bettina and I grow increasingly optimistic about my full recovery. Do I still face the threat of yet another relapse? Probably. But thanks to medical advances, physicians are able to detect imminent relapse sooner and treat it ever more effectively. As long as Andi remains able to leave Zurich at the drop of a hat and bring me his precious leukocytes or bone marrow, I feel confident that I will continue to live a productive, fulfilling life.

I am happy to say that I haven't been back to the leukemia ward since I recovered from my third bone-marrow transplant in fall 1998—at least not as a patient. But what I underwent there in 1991 affects me deeply to this day. The radiation treatment and chemotherapy I received had the same effect on my immune system as an all-out nuclear war would have on civilization: it sent the clock back to zero. Today, I have about the same level of resistance to infection as a twelve-year-old child. But whereas a normal child's immune system grows stronger every day, mine continues to this day to be very fragile. As such, I can't receive those vaccinations given to children to ward off a host of illnesses. To this day, I am unnerved whenever I hear that yet another new strain of flu has emerged, or that the latest version of the West Nile virus or SARS or monkey pox has jumped a plane and crossed the ocean.

Even though I love California and am endlessly glad that

Bettina and I chose to live here, the ever present sun is still not my friend. With its ability to initiate cancerous cell growth, sunlight poses as great a threat today as it did in 1991 when I walked out of my isolation room and into the full light of day for the first time in three months.

I continue to stay in touch with Drs. Kolb and Ledderose. For years now, they have been watching the progress of a group of CML patients in Seattle who have fought a battle similar to mine. All of these patients had allogeneic transplants using siblings' marrow when they were less than thirty years old and did so within one year of diagnosis. To date, 59 percent of the patients have been relapse-free for five years; 53 percent have done so for ten years. Those whose transplants have failed have had access to the DLI treatment, which in turn has had kept 70 percent of CML patients in remission.

Thanks to advances in medical technology, doctors are also able to examine human blood with ever greater resolution. Previously, physicians could spot the fateful signs of leukemic cells only when the Philadelphia chromosome-mutated cells were mature and in the hundreds per microliter of blood. Physicians can now spot them in lower concentrations—and at much earlier stages in their lifecycle.

The progress that has been made in the battle against leukemia has many heroes. Some come from the world of medicine. Beginning with Dr. E. Donnall Thomas and his researchers at the University of Washington and the Fred Hutchinson Cancer Research Center—and including the staff of Universitätsklinik Grosshadern Hospital—physicians, researchers, nurses, and orderlies have helped thousands of people like me survive chronic myeloid leukemia. For each patient, there are also the spouses, family members, and friends who provide support without which even the best medical treatments can be futile.

But there is one other hero, one who comes from the unlikely world of opera. Many citizens of the world know that José Carreras once battled leukemia. Fewer know that he has since raised and contributed many millions of dollars to both treat the current generation of patients and to advance research that may someday make leukemia a footnote in history.

Mr. Carreras's work has special meaning for Bettina and me. Determined to help those who came after him, the German José Carreras Leukemia Foundation donated more than $3 million to the Universitätsklinik Grosshadern, much of which was used to build a transplantation ward that now bears his name. Finished in 1997, the "José Carreras Transplantationseinheit" is the more advanced twin of my old ward, and is affectionately known as M21. Had this new facility been built ten years earlier when I was first diagnosed with CML, I would have had a different experience. As it was, I had to wait almost an entire year until the hospital had space for me. With a progressive disease such as leukemia, every moment of delay reduces a patient's chances of success. By doubling the number of beds for leukemia patients at Universitätsklinik Grosshadern, Carreras has brought new hope and new life to leukemia patients like me—and not like me. Doctors at my old hospital are now able to treat an increasing number of non-traditional patients, those who were once considered too old or too young, in too advanced a stage or with too complex a pathology. Now, thanks to Carreras, these patients can begin treating their cancer as soon as it is discovered.

Closest to our hearts will always be Professor Dr. Kolb, our friend Dr. George Ledderose, and the dedicated staff of Station L21. Not only did these people sustain me time after time when I thought my life would end—they also helped Bettina and me find meaning in a little piece of software, which has since found its own home in the world.

Epilogue: Bettina

IT IS A BRIGHT SUMMER MORNING as Mike and I walk out of our house and head for work. After a two-minute drive, we can see the one hundred fifty-foot tall chimney that marks Mindjet's newest headquarters. The smokestack is all that remains of a factory that at the turn of the century fired the bricks that rebuilt an earthquake-ravaged San Francisco. It somehow seems fitting that we ended up here, because our story is all about rebuilding, too.

Years ago, when we first began planning our future, Mike and I imagined a life very different life from the one we now lead. But strange as it might seem to say, we are in many ways thankful for Mike's disease. How could we not be? It brought our families together in a way that only adversity can. It opened our eyes to strengths we never knew we had. It brought us this business. But most important, it taught us how to build a life that each day reflects our innermost values. What we learned during our Bone Marrow Olympics training days is with us now. While it is wonderful to see Mindjet grow, our deep satisfaction comes from treasuring family and friends, honoring our bodies and our minds, taking time to relax, and keeping in perspective those things that might once have pushed us into fits of anger, frustration, or sorrow. I guess you could say that all these years after Mike woke up in pain one Christmas morning, we feel like we have finally graduated from an incredibly extensive course in counting one's blessings.

We drive another three minutes, past the grassy golden hills of Marin to the left and Larkspur Landing to the right, and arrive at work. While my parents have yet to visit our newest offices, they've seen our pictures. They are happy to know that while I now live on the other side of the planet, I haven't really strayed that far away after all. All day long, the ferries chug back and forth below my window, braving summer winds and winter rains—all the while causing me to remember how far my husband and I have come from Bavaria.

Acknowledgements

We would like to express our gratitude to our family and friends for their love and encouragement and all the moments we have shared together, and all those yet to come: Roland and Lydia Jetter, Ulrike Jetter and Peter Kremer, Frederik, Lucia, Andi and Ruth Jetter, Viola, Josef and Therese Pauli, Diana Pauli, Nicole Pauli, the Bone Marrow Transplant Olympic Team: (Uli, Karin Fürsich, Reinhard Klein, Christine Schramm), Andi und Evi Kisslinger, Marion Dersch, Catja Klein, Lorainne Habdank and Stefan Jedlitschka, Hans and Andrea Hölzl, Stefan and Andrea Hölzl, Jutta Reinhardt, Hannolore Rasch, Lindner family, Michael and Birgit Korbonitz, Franz Buchenberger, Robert and Susan Schöller, Peter and Tamiko Graf, Thilo Schwertfeger, Rolf and Gundel Werner, Vogels, Robert Rank, Christoph Frank, Hilli and Heiner Riegler, Edith and Wolfram Kudla, Shelley Baldridge.

We wish to thank a number of people who have made major contributions to the growth of Mindjet: Michael Louis, Chris Holmes, Wolfgang Männel, Nicolas von der Schulenburg. **Mindjet US:** Adam Willett, Amy Melton, Amy Palmer, Andrew Mochalskyy, Anthony Roy, Bruce Bowers, Catherine Ogilvie, Dale and Ute Berman, Don Souza, Donna Trauger, Erik Harvell, Francoise Johnson, Giovanna Vitau, Hobart Swan, Igor Shirokov, Inna Kuchmekno, James Saito, Janice Butler, Jeanne Daniele, Jeanne Sperry, Jin Gong, Jochen van der Mühlen, Kathleen Marmion, Kristin Hersant, Kristin Tsuchimoto, Larry Daniele, Licia Hayden, Lisa Goldstein, Lisa Ricci, Lucja Kwasniak, Marie MacKay,　Matthew O'Brien, Michael Zaydman, Michael Scherotter, Ming Chi Tsai, Nick Duffill, Olin Reams, Peter Hizalev, Rachel Tallant, Sandra Vögeli, Stefan Funk, Stein Asmul, Teri Rogers, Tim Madrid, Tom Blossom, Youlanda Pieri. **Mindjet Europe:** Albrecht Ackermann, Andre Kress, Andrea Wohlschlogel, Antje Louis, Armin Schneider, Bernd Laskowski, Bernhard Straub, Bettina Mathis, Carmen Teichmann, Christoph

Hodapp, Cornelia Barthel, Dagmar Herzog, Daniela Gallo, Dirk Blume, Gabi Bittel, Gudrun Schuhmacher, Janine Ebneth, Jochen Barop, Jochen Kraft, Jörg Steiss, Karsten Rühe, Katrin Engel, Kirsten Thayer, Klaus Roth, Klaus-Peter Frömel, Matthias Heiss, Mojca Peklaj, Nathalie Narrog, Neshat Falakfarsa, Norbert Schuster, Pascale Narrog, Steven Bashford, Ursula Baier, Yvonne Brill, Mindjet UK: Peter Bragg, Richard Watts.

We are also grateful that we have crossed paths with the following people who have become such great evangelists of our product—extraordinary people all: John England, Cliff Shaffran, Bo Seiffert, Eric Greenberg, David Hill, Al Holmyk, Debby McIssac, Wendy Wallbridge, Cynthia LaForge, Bernd Wobser, Günter Kugel, Helmut Abbenhard, Jim Winninger, Jim Hope, Peter Meinen, Uli Kan, Hans Maenner, Bernd Schlüter, Gerd Zöttlein, Marty Fox, Peter Veiser, Preben Gammelmark, Tony Buzan, Vanda North, Sigi and Pauline Siegrist, Lawrence Webb, Tony Dottino, Rick Hamilton, Ron Glickman, Bernard Clark, Dan Kusnetzky, Daniel Rasmus.

Special thanks to editor Constance Hale for her endless and endlessly useful suggestions and ideas, Mandy Erickson for carefully parsing of our manuscript, Anne Irving for hundreds of pages of unfailingly accurate transcriptions, Hobart Swan for compressing thirteen years of our lives into one coherent story, Gina Bessire for her perseverance and frequent single-parenting throughout the project, and Olive Swan for being patient with her dad.

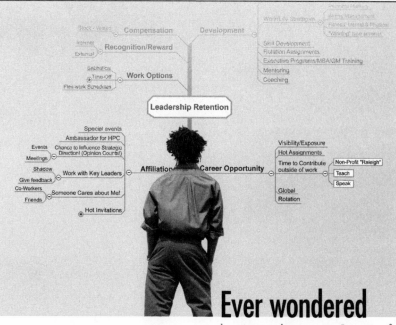